AROUND THE WORLD IN

80 DRAWINGS

Around the World in 80 Drawings

by A.S. House

Illustrated by Rebecca Warfel

Let your pencil lead you on an amazing journey,
with tips and inspiration along the way

Table of Contents

CONCLUSION

Introduction

- ## Purpose of this book:

  Congratulations! You are now the proud owner of *Around the World in 80 Drawings*. You may have picked up this book for a number of reasons: maybe the catchy title caught your attention; maybe you are interested in learning how to draw landscapes, or perhaps you enjoy traveling and are looking for inspiration through sketching. Whether you plan to physically travel the world with this book in hand, or if you prefer to be whisked away in you imagination to one of the magnifcent locations, I hope I can deliver on your expectations.

  Many drawing books aim to teach you how to draw by explaining the aspects of size, placement, overlapping and shading. Often times, these books get very technically detailed and others oversimplify. My target is to find a happy medium with this book by providing useful tips on how to tackle your drawings, without digging too deep into the technical aspects of sketching. In addition to sketching tips throughout the pages, I have included a brief list of what I like to call "fun facts" about each location; you'll also find a sample sketch to inspire your creative side. Don't feel like you are limited to follow the sample sketches, or copy the medium used. I want you to express your creativity, and be your own artist. Whether abstract or geometrical, creativity is encouraged!

- ## Tools:

  First things first, as you thumb through the pages of this book, you may notice the even numbered pages are left mainly blank apart from a small amount of text labeled "Tips". No, I have not cheated you out of half of the book; instead, I have allocated space for you to actually draw your artwork in this book! However, drawing in a book sometimes puts people off as they feel they are defacing it. Maybe you would like to go back and do the sketch again, or perhaps you would like to loan this book out and keep possession of your sketches. If this sounds like you, and you prefer not to draw directly on the pages, or if you have purchased this book on an eReader, you are welcome to use your favorite sketchpad alongside the book and still receive the same benefits.

  Now that we have a drawing surface covered (either the empty pages or your sketchbook), let's look at the other basic tools I would recommend as you work your way through this book.

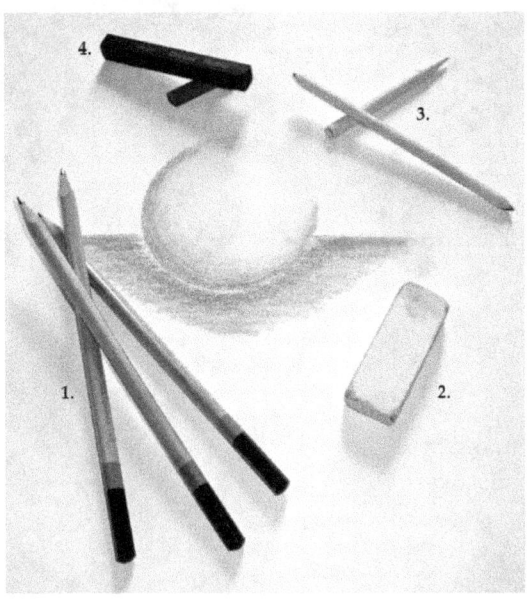

1. A pencil set with different shades is helpful, but not mandatory. The lower the number of the pencil, the darker the mark will be.

2. A quality eraser, if not several, are important to ensure you don't damage the quality of the paper. In this example you can see a white gum eraser, but a kneaded eraser or mechanical eraser can also be useful.

3. Assorted blending stumps and tortillions (shading tool) to allow you to blend shading in both large and small areas.

4. Charcoal sticks are also an alternative medium that can be used.

For ease of sketching, a generic ruler and pencil sharpener are welcomed tools that are not included in the image. Lastly, do not limit your creativity to the tools listed above. Feel free to explore additional mediums such as watercolors, paint, etc.

▪ Map of represented countries:

I hope this book sparks some creativity in you, while you learn something interesting about the 80 global locations which fill the pages. For your convenience, I have included a map below of all the countries represented throughout *Around the World in 80 Drawings* (countries present are colored in black). Enjoy you trip!

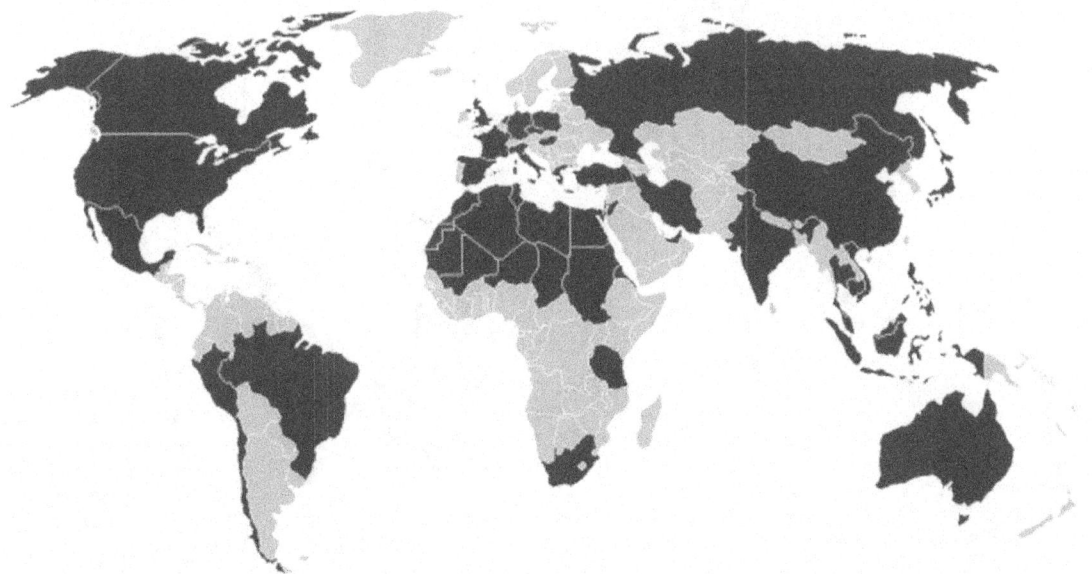

* *Antarctica represented, but not present on map*

Alcazar of Segovia

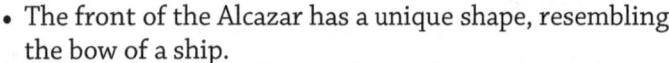

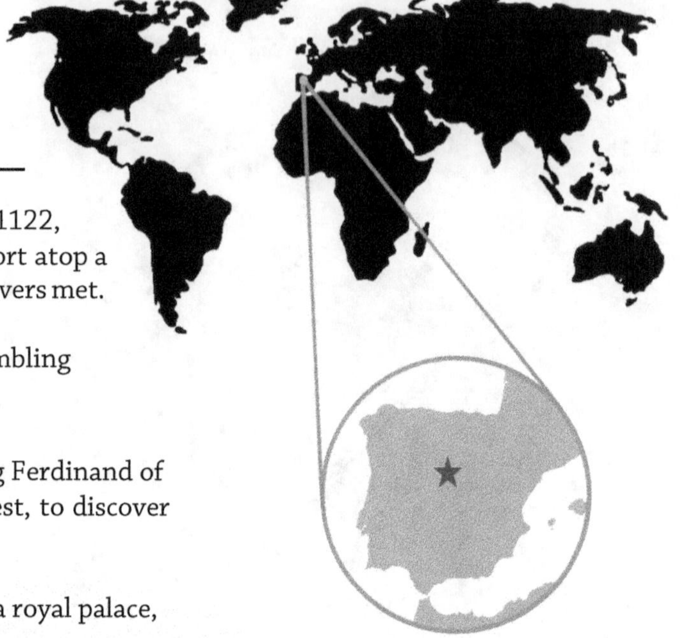

- The first mention of the Alcazar of Segovia was in 1122, where the structure was described as a wooden fort atop a rocky cliff-face where the Eresma and Clamores Rivers met.

- The front of the Alcazar has a unique shape, resembling the bow of a ship.

- It was once the home of Queen Isabella I and King Ferdinand of Spain, who sent Christopher Columbus to the west, to discover the "New World".

- Over its lifetime, the Alcazar has been a fortress, a royal palace, a state prison, a Royal Artillery School, as well as a military college.

- The Alcazar is the oldest of several castles that inspired the look of Cinderella's castle in Disney World, Florida.

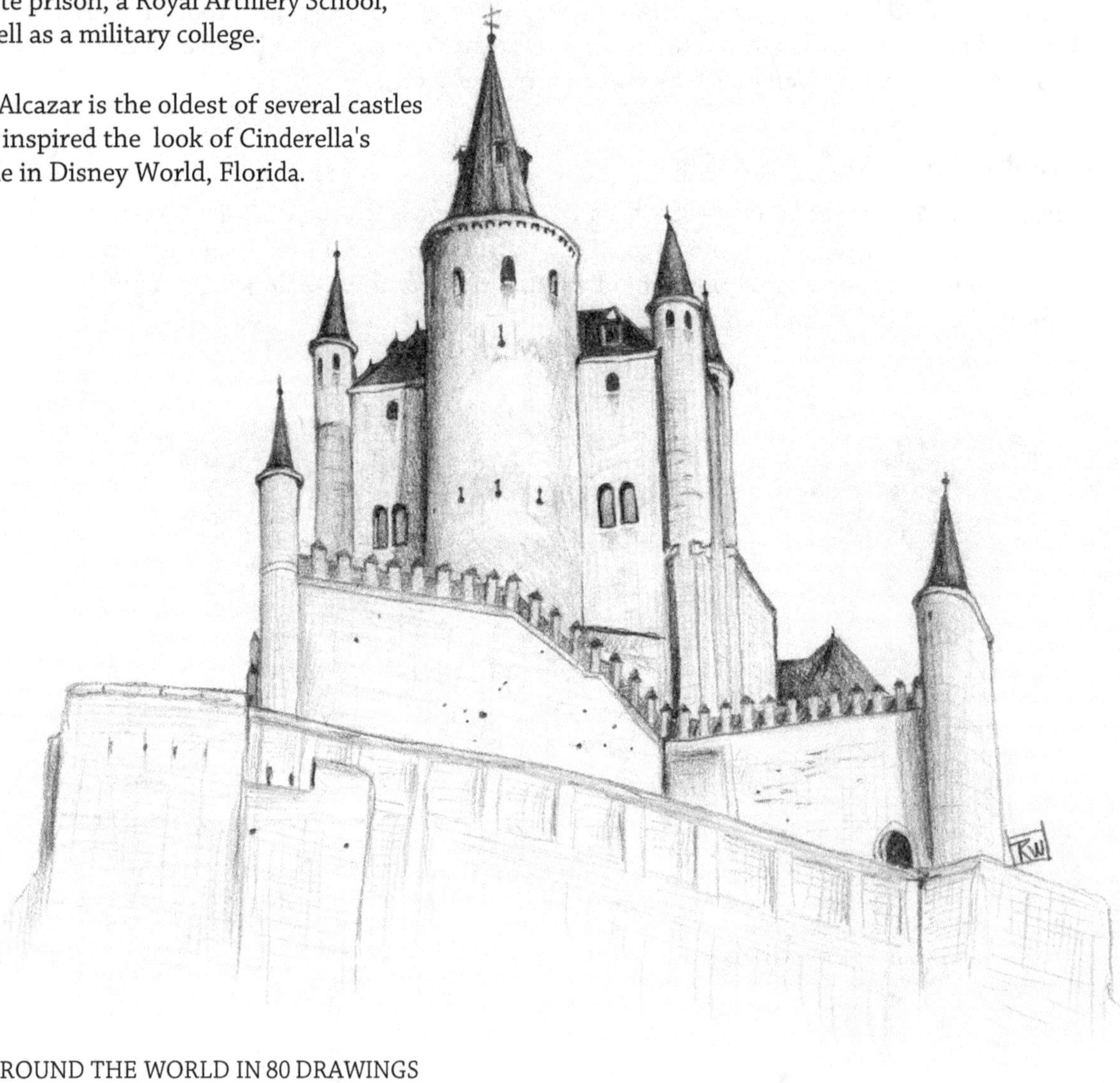

TIP:
Hold the pencil in a way that's most comfortable.
Long sessions of sketching can give your hand a cramp.
Take breaks whenever your hand gets tired.

Amalfi Coast

- It is said that an Italian mariner named Flavio Gioa, from Amalfi invented the compass. However, turns out, Flavio Gioa was a person who never actually existed!

- Due to contact with Arab cultures, Amalfi was one of the first places in Europe where modern day paper was made.

- Up until the 19th century, accessing the Amalfi coast by land necessitated the use of mules for transportation due to the rugged terrain.

- The Li Galli islands off the coast of the Sorrento peninsula are said to be the home to Sirens from *The Odyssey* by Homer. The Sirens would tempt and distract sailors who would then crash their ships into the rocky islands.

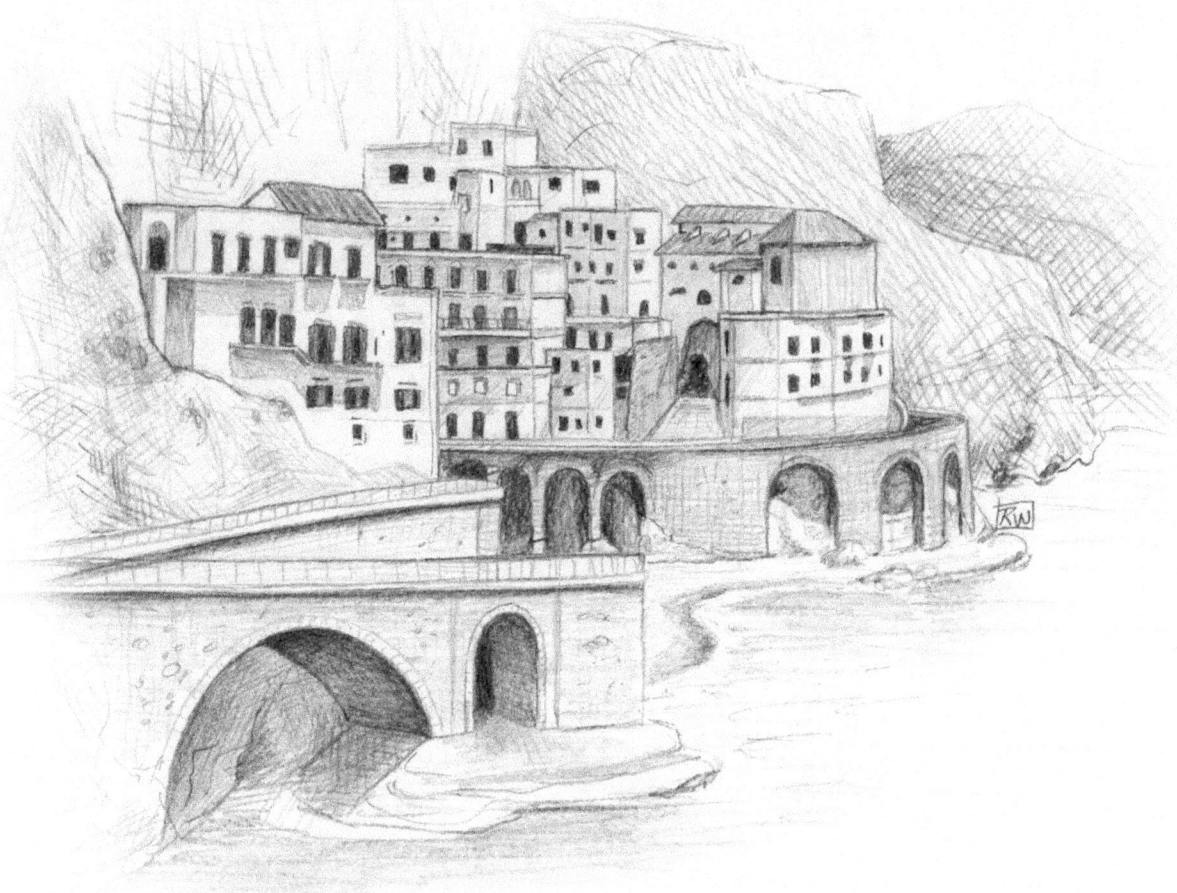

TIP:
Draw the details that you want to be the focal point of the sketch. Give them the most clarity.

Angkor Wat

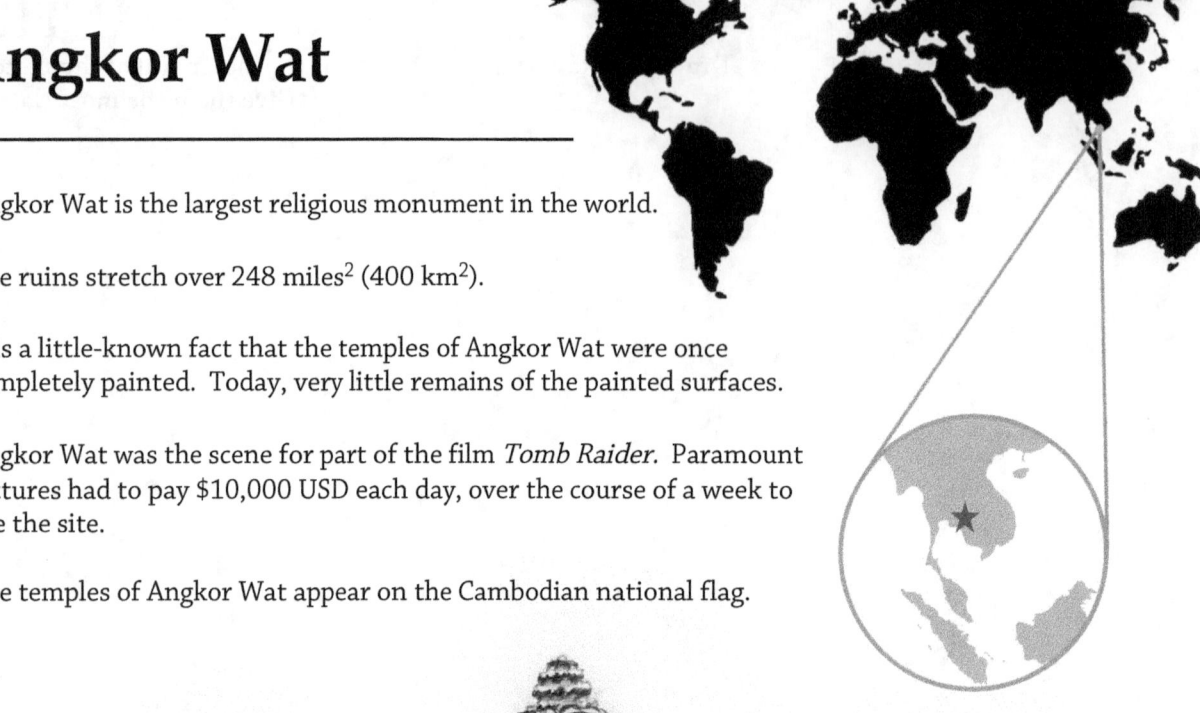

- Angkor Wat is the largest religious monument in the world.

- The ruins stretch over 248 miles^2 (400 km^2).

- It is a little-known fact that the temples of Angkor Wat were once completely painted. Today, very little remains of the painted surfaces.

- Angkor Wat was the scene for part of the film *Tomb Raider*. Paramount Pictures had to pay $10,000 USD each day, over the course of a week to use the site.

- The temples of Angkor Wat appear on the Cambodian national flag.

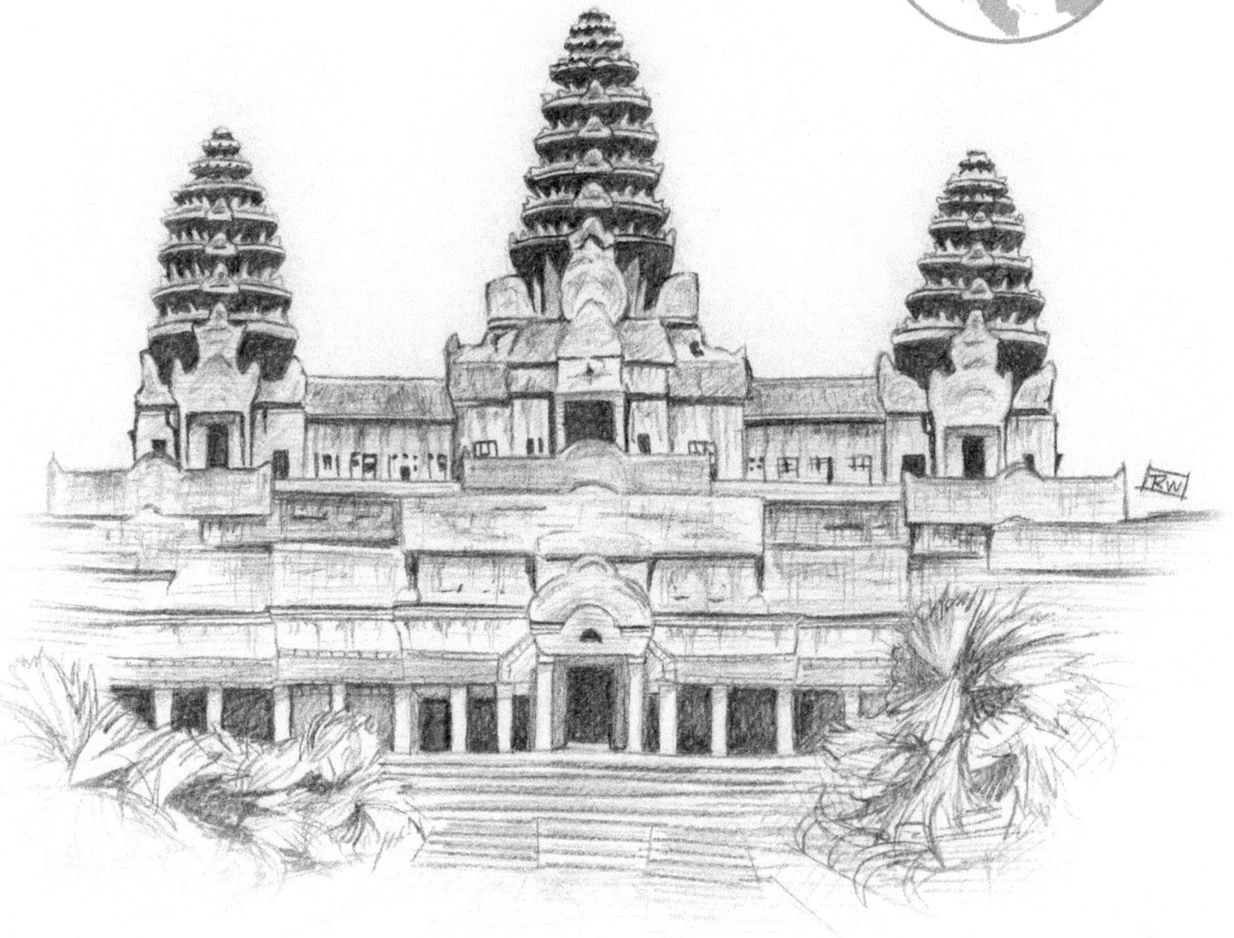

TIP:

Sometimes it's easier to use a darker pencil first, to block in the deepest shadows. Then go back in with other shading.

Arch of Triumph

- The Arch of Triumph was commissioned by Napoleon Bonaparte in 1806 and took 30 years to complete.

- Although Napoleon was never able to see the finished Arch (completed 15 years after his death), his body did pass through it in 1840, on its way to Les Invalides, his final resting place.

- The Arch of Triumph sits at the center of the well-known Place de Charles or Place de l'Étoile, which is the meeting point for 12 straight avenues, thus making the shape of a star.

- The Arch stands as a rallying point for French soldiers parading on Bastille Day (France's Independence Day).

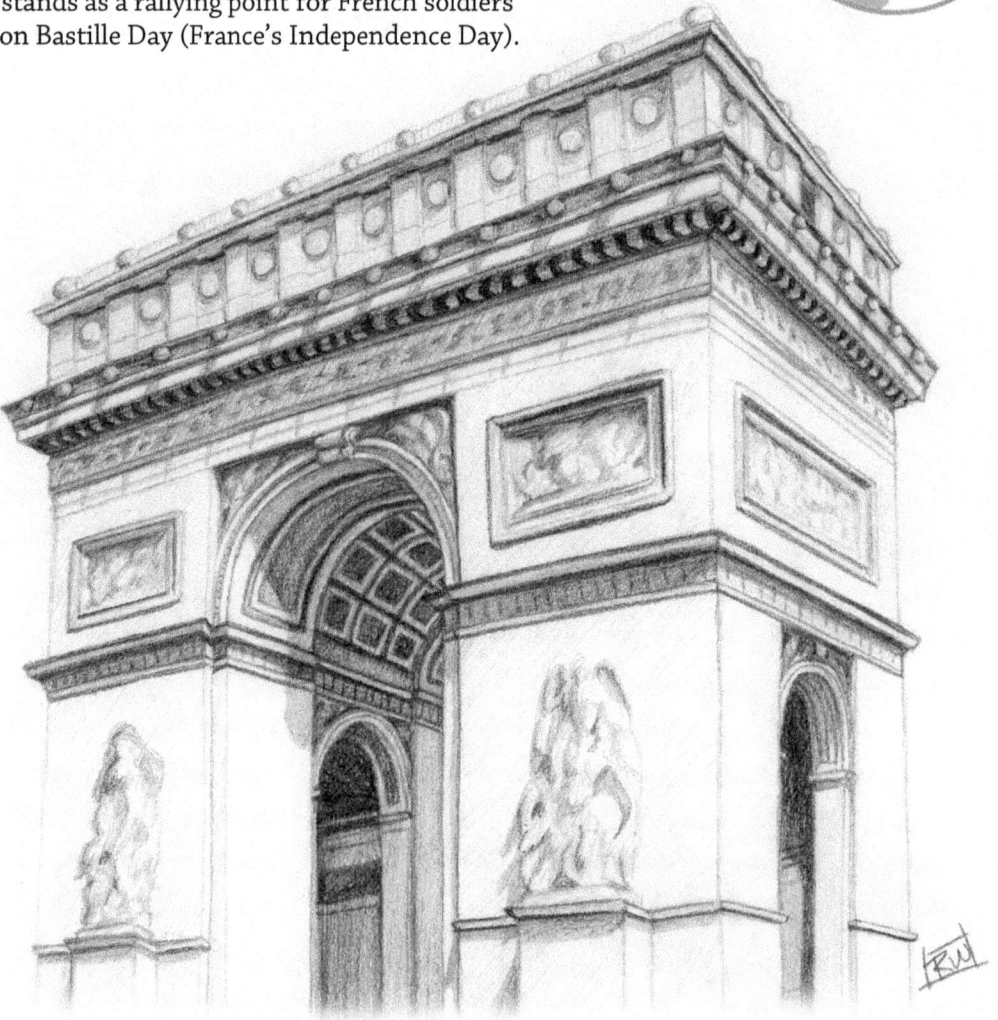

Banaue Rice Terraces

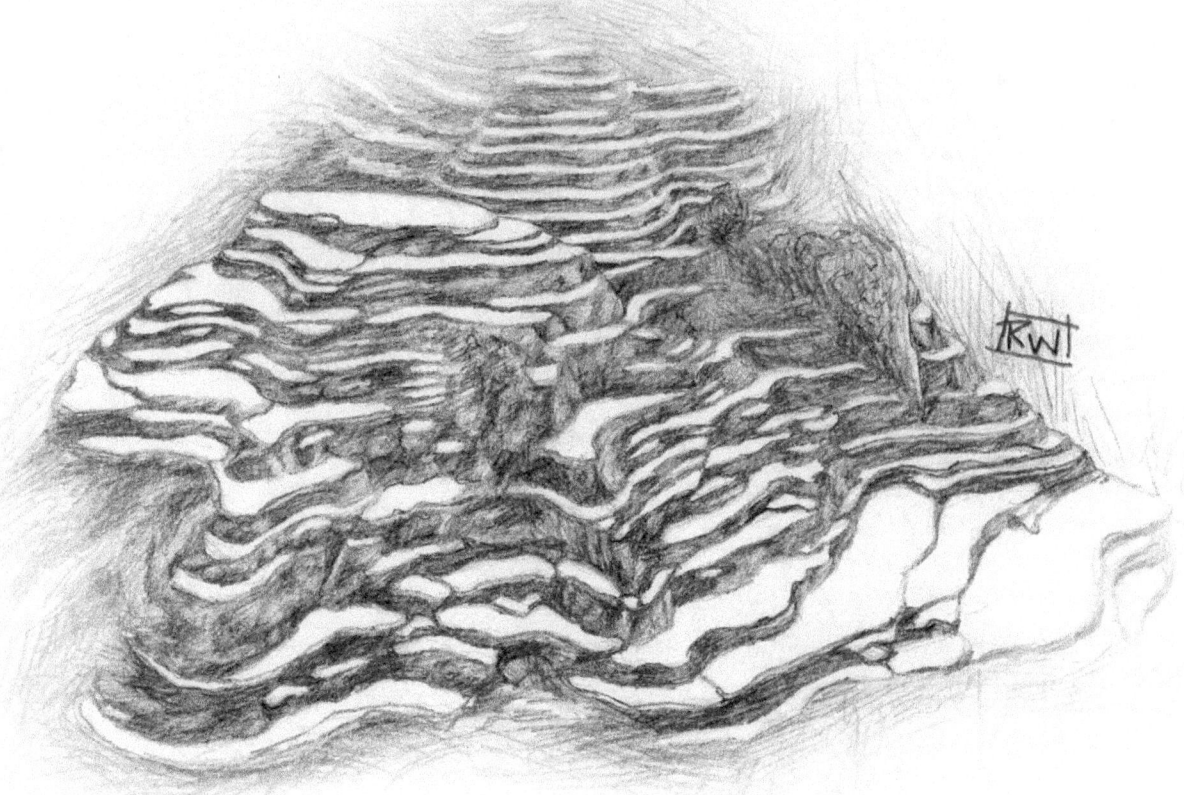

- The Banaue Rice Terraces were built over 2,000 years ago by the Ifugao people of the Philippines.

- The terraces are considered to be one of the greatest engineering achievements of men. They were manually constructed by the indigenous people, using rocks, crude implements, and their bare hands to transform the rugged Cordillera Mountains into useable land on which to grow rice and other vegetables.

- It has been said, if you took all the tiers of the steps and put them next to each other, it would encircle half of the world.

- The rice terraces are irrigated using a traditional, ancient irrigation system from the rainforests above the terraces.

- The Filipinos consider the Banaue Rice Terraces as the "8th Wonder of the World".

TIP:

Block shading, or using flat shades of solid lights and darks, is sometimes best to sketch certain forms.

Big Ben

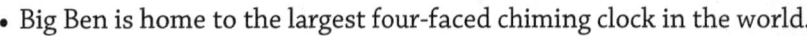

- The tower adjoined to the British Houses of Parliament is nicknamed "Big Ben", but it is actually formally called the "Clock Tower" or the "Elizabeth Tower" (renamed in 2012 to honor the Diamond Jubilee of Queen Elizabeth II).

- Big Ben is home to the largest four-faced chiming clock in the world.

- The largest bell in the clock tower is affectionately named "Big Ben" in honor of Sir Benjamin Hall, who oversaw the installation of the bell. Nowadays, the name refers to the bell, and by extension the tower and clock.

- The clock is famous for its reliability due to its unique pendulum (which is housed inside the tower). The rate of the pendulum swing is calibrated by a small stack of pennies that sits on the pendulum. The addition or removal of a single penny will change the clock's speed by 0.4 second/day.

- The clock tower sits at a tilt due to the excavations for the Westminster tube station in the 1990s. It leans northwest by 9.1 inches and is now viewable to the naked eye.

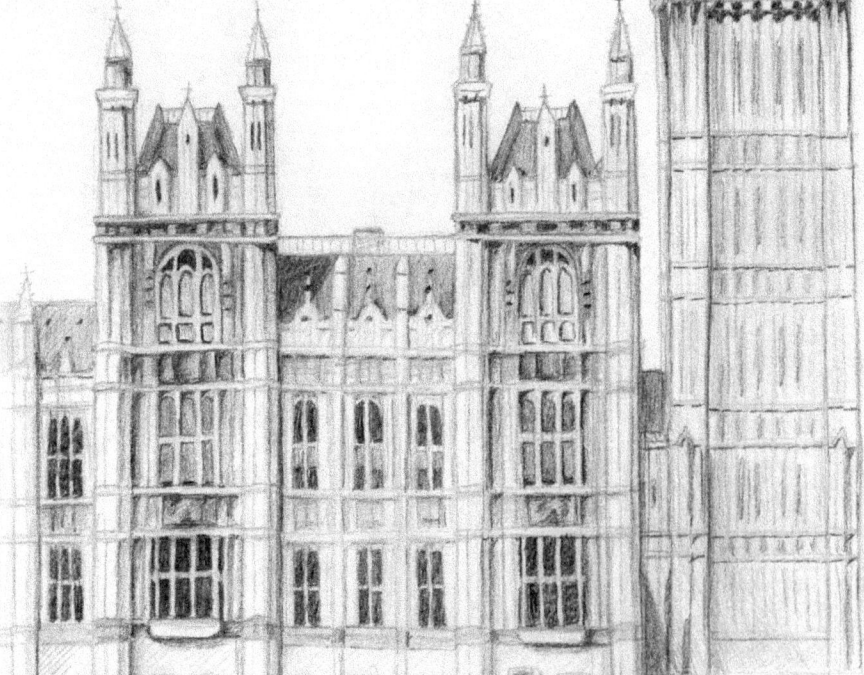

If the structure has a lot of detail, it's easier to sketch light lines before shading; like an outline.

Blue Mosque

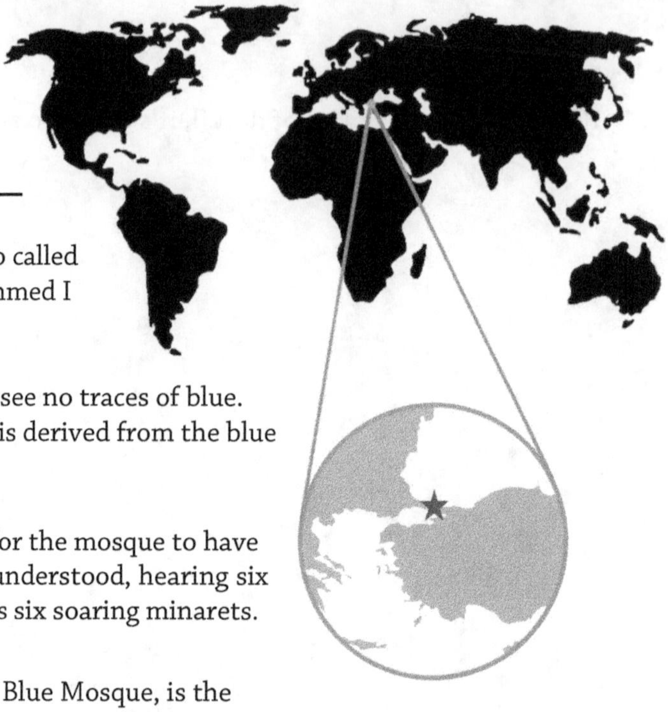

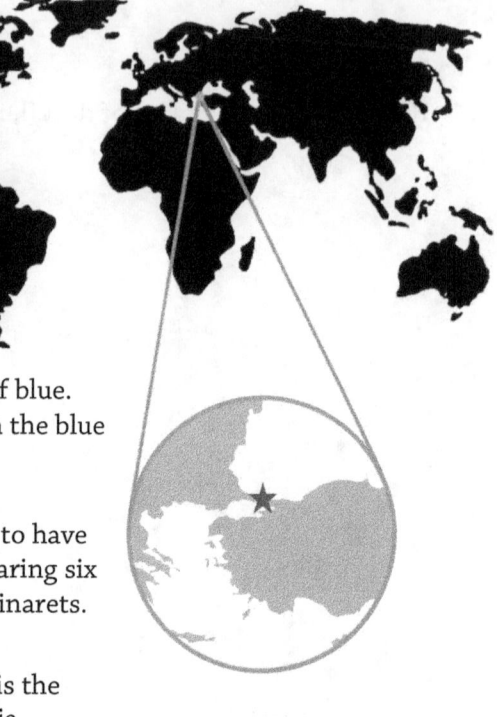

- Although it is known as the Blue Mosque, it is also called the Sultan Ahmed Mosque; named after Sultan Ahmed I who commissioned the build.

- If you look at the exterior of the mosque, you will see no traces of blue. Why is it called the Blue Mosque then? The name is derived from the blue tiles that adorn the interior.

- It is said that during the design the Sultan asked for the mosque to have gold (altin) minarets. However, the architect misunderstood, hearing six (alti) minarets, and thus the finished structure has six soaring minarets.

- The city of Istanbul, Turkey, which is home to the Blue Mosque, is the only city in the world that sits on two continents: Europe and Asia

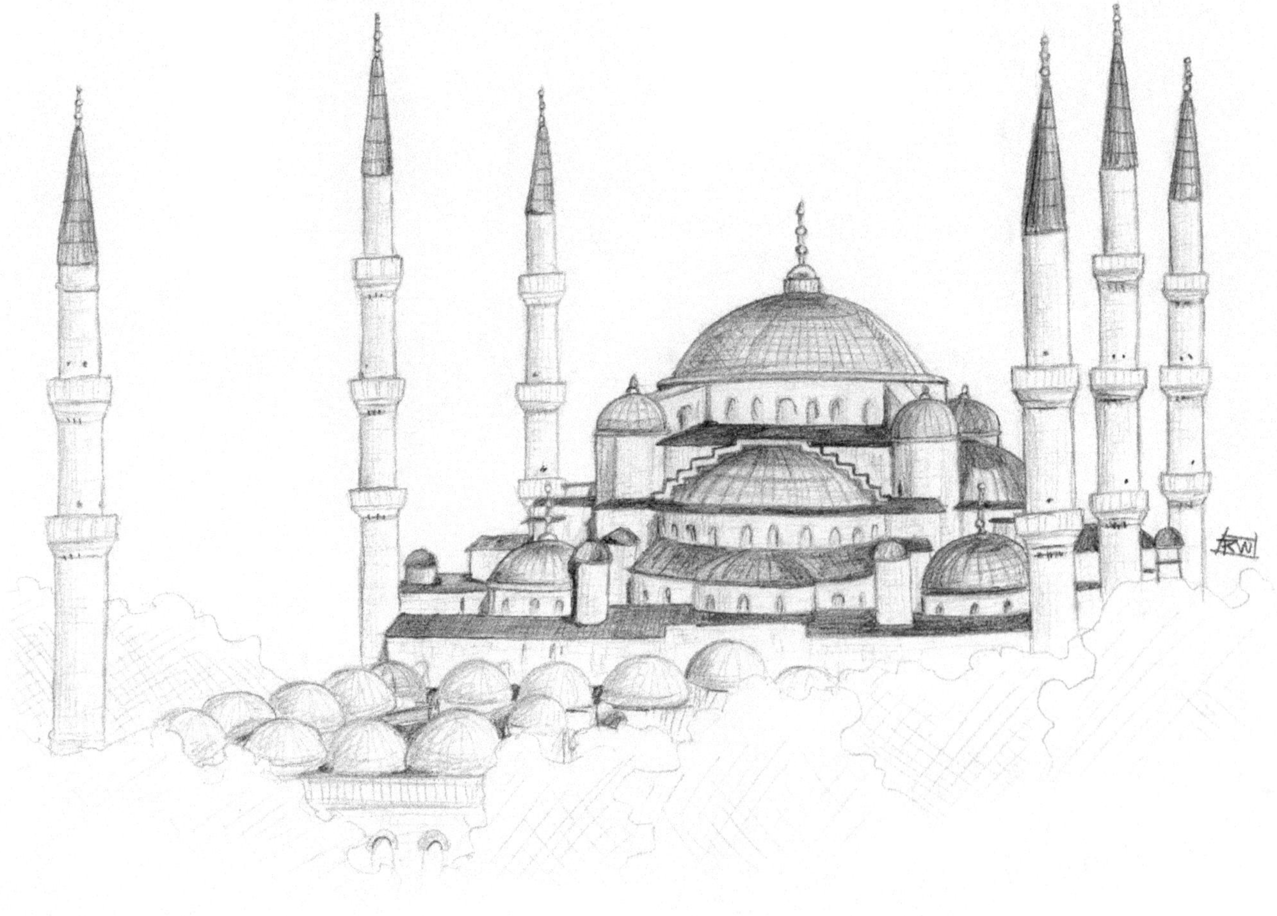

When shading objects that are rounded, curve the sketch lines to create a sense of depth and shape.

Borobudur

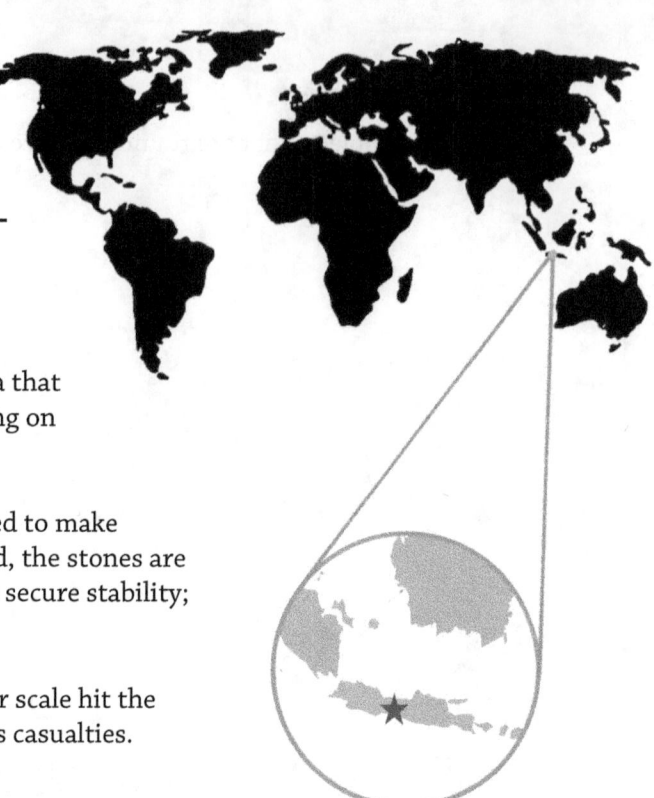

- The Borobudur temple was built between 778 and 842 AD.

- Borobudur is decorated with 504 statues of Buddha that demonstrate six different hand positions, depending on their placement throughout the monument

- Although over two million volcanic stones were used to make the enormous structure, there is no mortar. Instead, the stones are interlocked with a system of dovetails and joints to secure stability; like a giant puzzle!

- In 2006, a 6.2 magnitude earthquake on the Richter scale hit the area causing severe damage to the regions as well as casualties. Luckily, Borobudur remained undamaged.

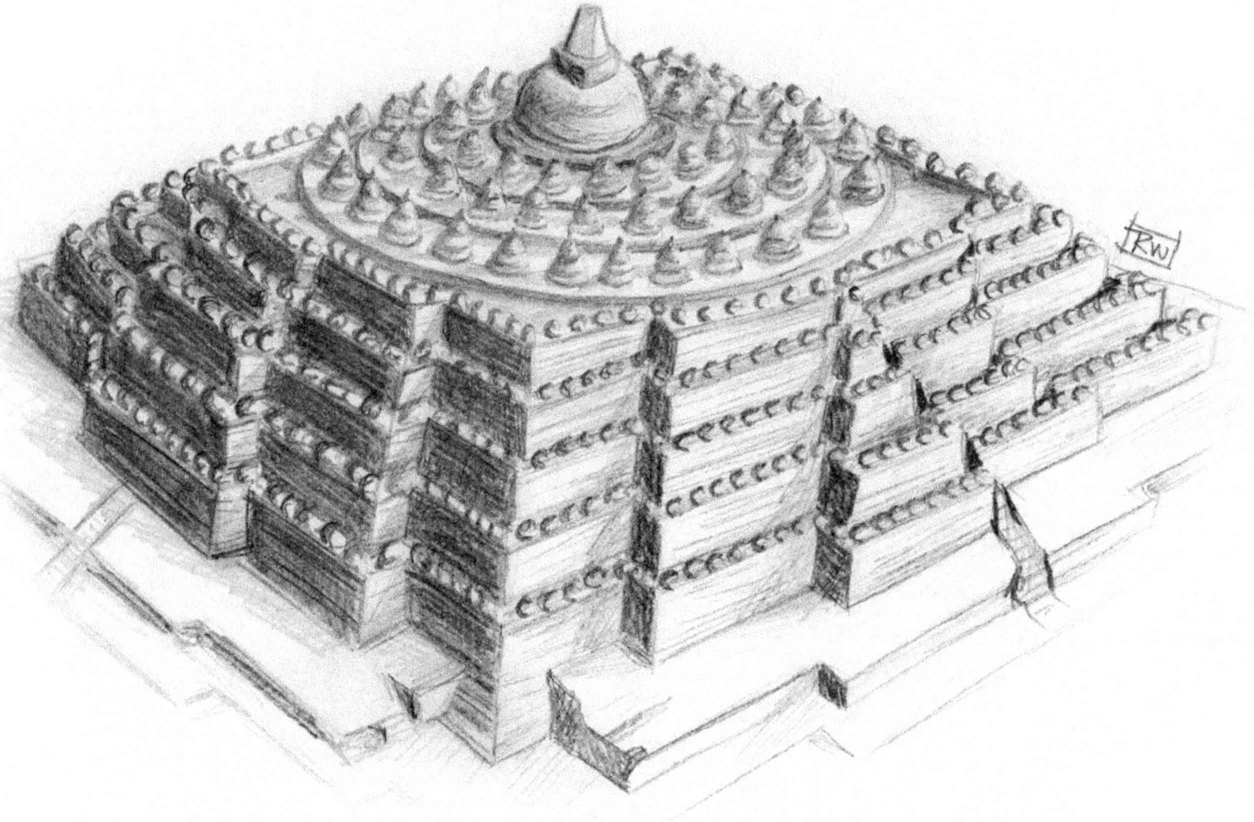

When there are too many small details on a large structure, simplify as best as you can.

Brandenburg Gate

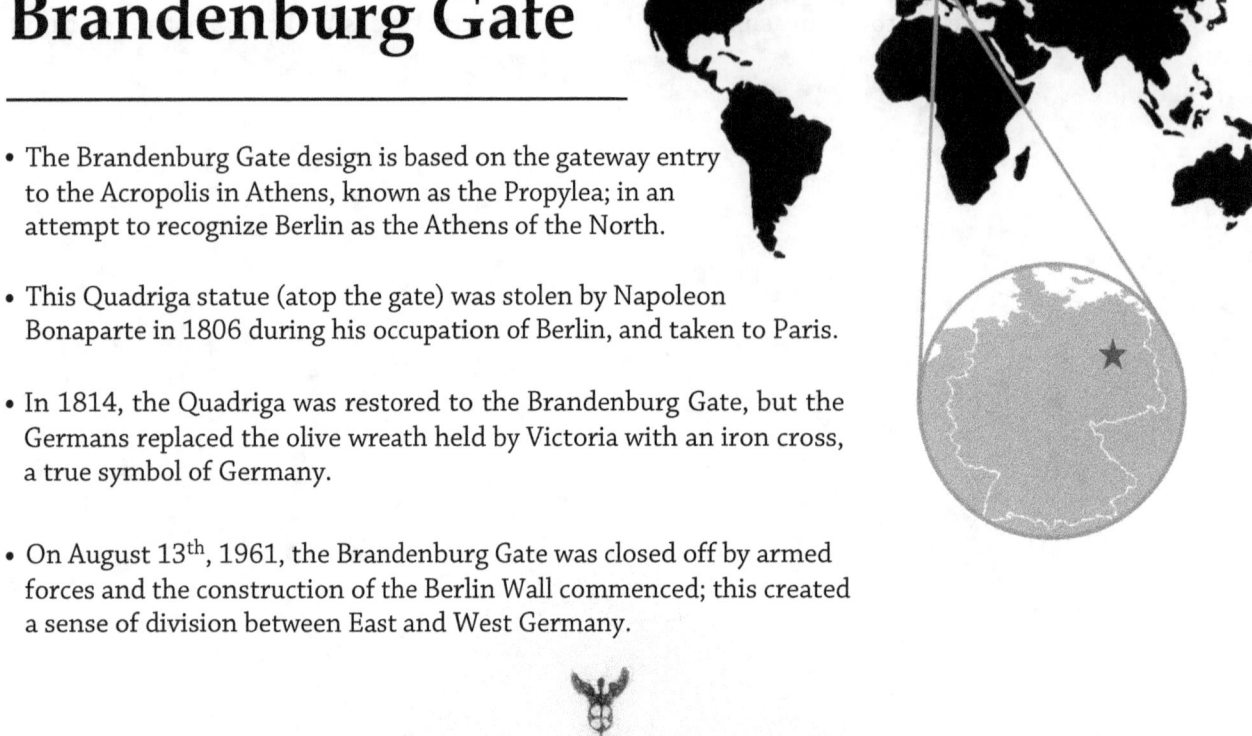

- The Brandenburg Gate design is based on the gateway entry to the Acropolis in Athens, known as the Propylea; in an attempt to recognize Berlin as the Athens of the North.

- This Quadriga statue (atop the gate) was stolen by Napoleon Bonaparte in 1806 during his occupation of Berlin, and taken to Paris.

- In 1814, the Quadriga was restored to the Brandenburg Gate, but the Germans replaced the olive wreath held by Victoria with an iron cross, a true symbol of Germany.

- On August 13th, 1961, the Brandenburg Gate was closed off by armed forces and the construction of the Berlin Wall commenced; this created a sense of division between East and West Germany.

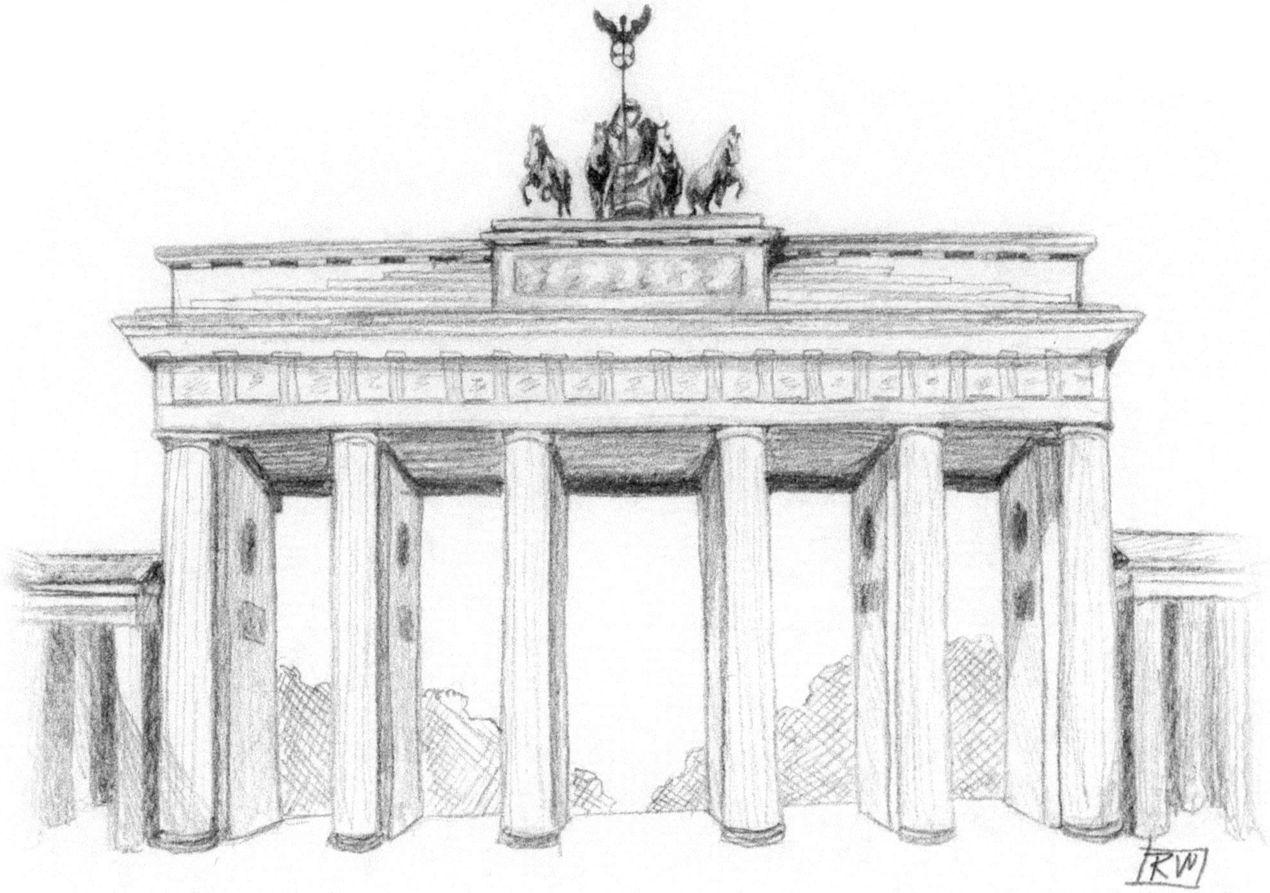

Don't be afraid to go over marks already made to darken them into shadows or distinct lines.

Brooklyn Bridge

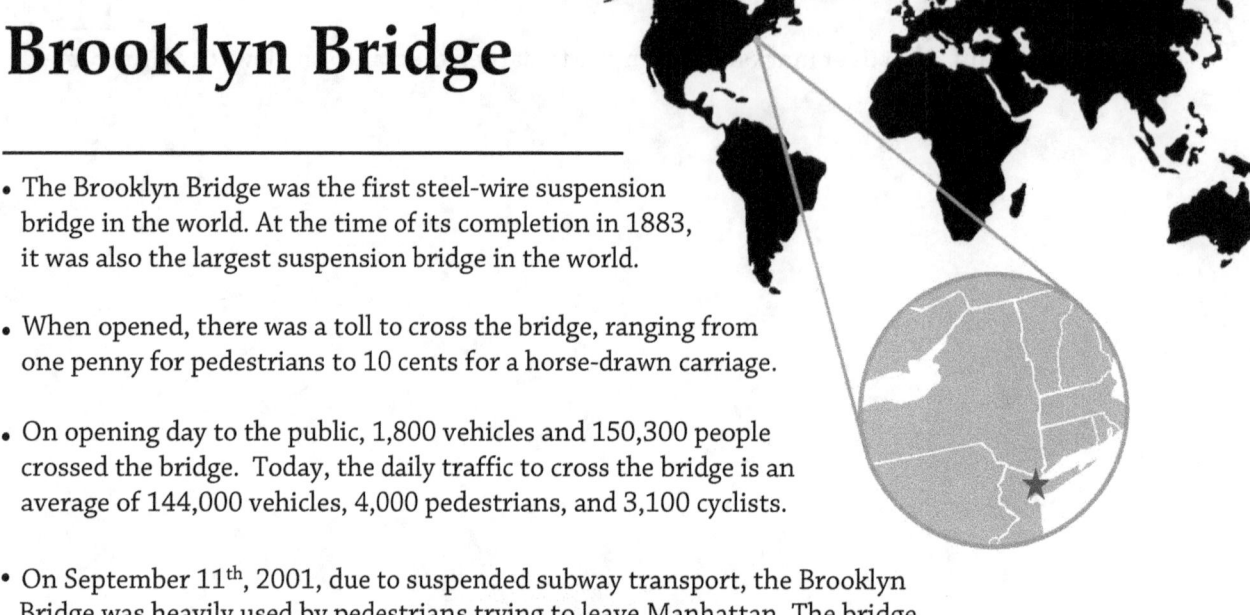

- The Brooklyn Bridge was the first steel-wire suspension bridge in the world. At the time of its completion in 1883, it was also the largest suspension bridge in the world.

- When opened, there was a toll to cross the bridge, ranging from one penny for pedestrians to 10 cents for a horse-drawn carriage.

- On opening day to the public, 1,800 vehicles and 150,300 people crossed the bridge. Today, the daily traffic to cross the bridge is an average of 144,000 vehicles, 4,000 pedestrians, and 3,100 cyclists.

- On September 11th, 2001, due to suspended subway transport, the Brooklyn Bridge was heavily used by pedestrians trying to leave Manhattan. The bridge was not designed to handle an increased load and was reported to sway.

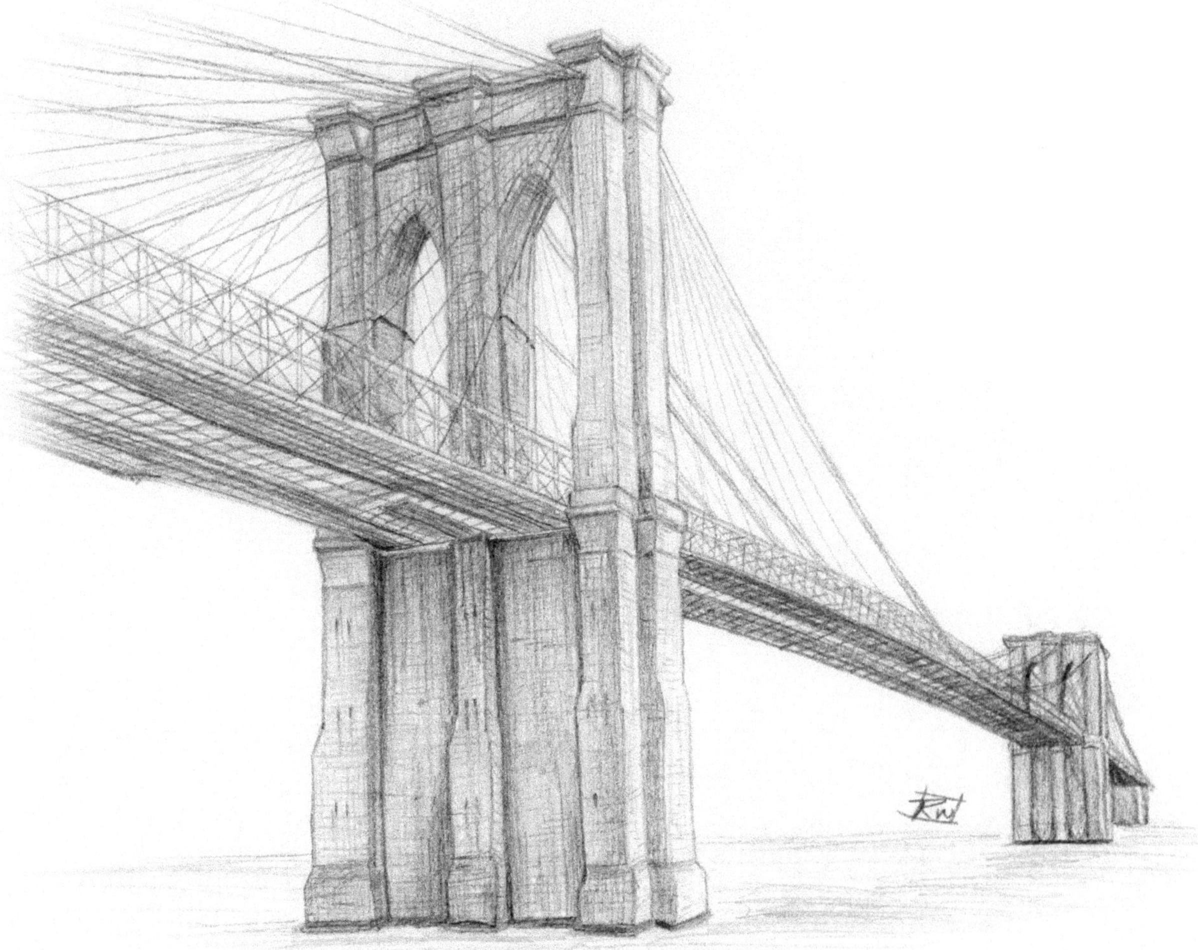

Use a ruler when sketching structures with longer perspective; it's not always necessary, but it helps.

Buckingham Palace

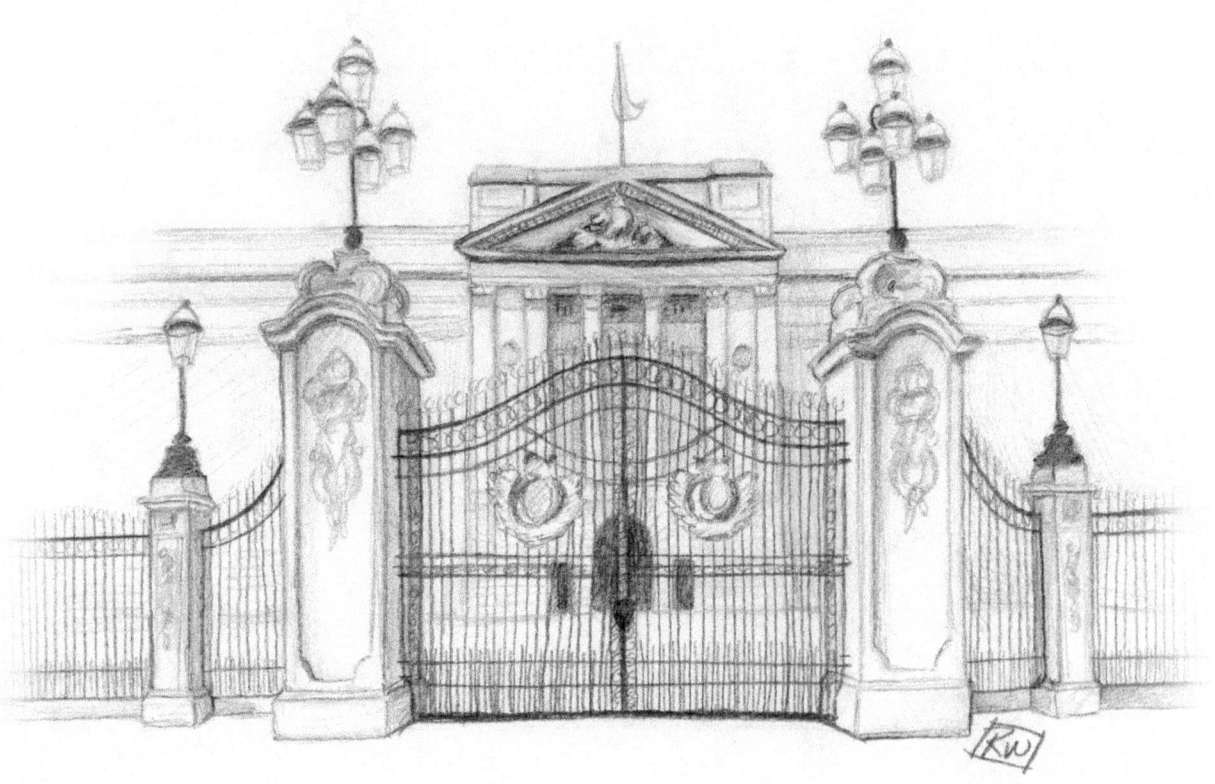

- The site of Buckingham Palace was previously a mulberry garden planted by King James I to raise silkworms. Unfortunately, the wrong mulberry bushes were chosen and silk production never took place.

- Buckingham Palace has 775 rooms, 1,514 doors, and 760 windows. The windows are cleaned every six weeks.

- Buckingham Palace is home to one of the largest collections of working clocks. There are more than 350 clocks and watches in the palace, which are maintained and wound every week by two full-time horologists.

- There is always a flag present above Buckingham Palace. The Royal Standard flies when the Queen is present, otherwise, the Union Flag will be on display.

- During World War II, Buckingham Palace suffered nine direct bomb hits.

TIP:

Sketch lightly at first, pressing gently on the paper.
This makes it easier to erase mistakes.

Burj Al Arab

- The Burj Al Arab hotel is built on a man-made island constructed roughly 305 yards (280 meters) off the Jumeirah shore. To establish a solid foundation, concrete piles were driven into the sand and the friction of the sand and silt along the length of the piles supports the structure.

- During the day, the public areas of the hotel are lit only by natural light.

- There are 29,000 Swarovski crystals in the ceiling of Junsui Lounge, designed in the shape of the Milky Way.

- The Burj Al Arab is one of the most expensive hotels in the world, with suites ranging from $1,000 to $28,000 USD per night!

Use gradation in your shading on metallic or glass surfaces – going from light to dark and back again.

Chichen Itza

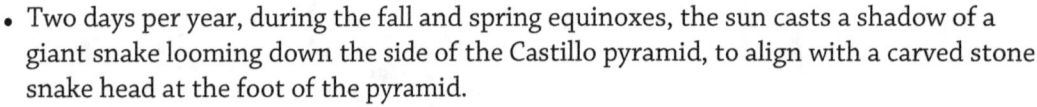

- Chichen Itza is located near two large sinkholes, which made for an attractive location for the Mayan people to settle. They would have used the sinkholes as a water source.

- It's believed that one of the sinkholes, known as the Sacred Cenote, was used as a place of human sacrifice to honor Chac, the rain god.

- The Castillo pyramid is full of cosmological symbolism. Its four sides contain 365 steps (symbolizing each day in the solar year) and 52 panels (depicting each week of the solar year, and each year in the Mayan century).

- Two days per year, during the fall and spring equinoxes, the sun casts a shadow of a giant snake looming down the side of the Castillo pyramid, to align with a carved stone snake head at the foot of the pyramid.

- It's unknown why the people of Chichen Itza abandoned the city for the jungle in the 1400s; artwork and architecture were left behind, with no documented reason as to why. It is speculated that droughts, overused soils, and quests for treasure are some of the possibe reasons for desertion.

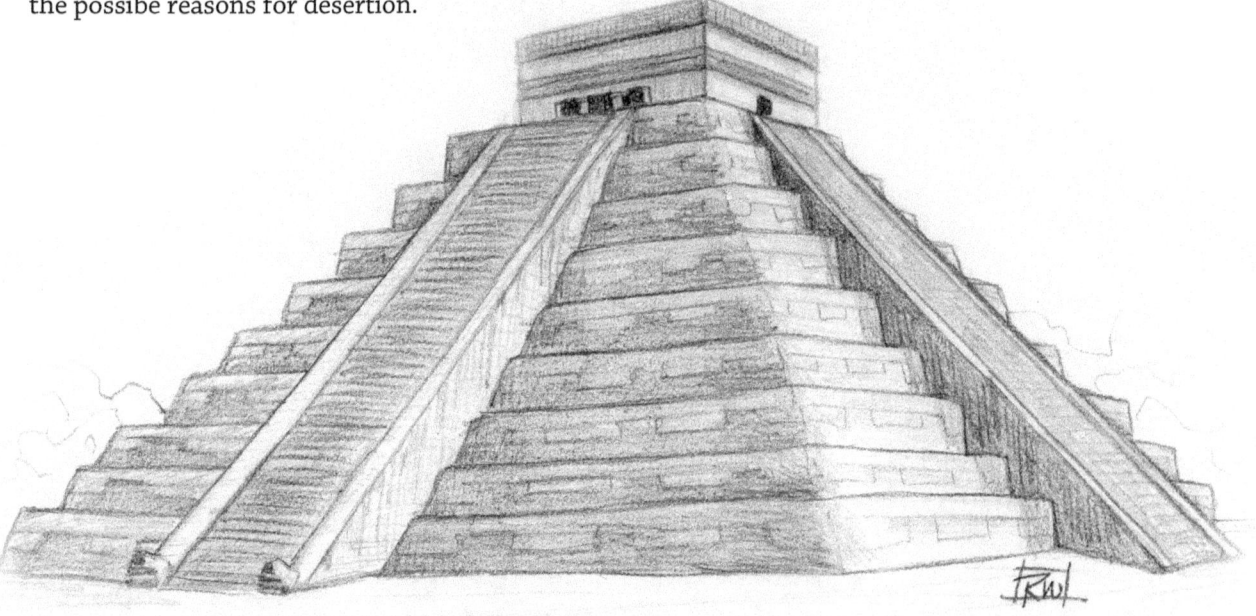

TIP:

Always sign your work, especially if it's a piece that you particularly like.

Christ the Redeemer

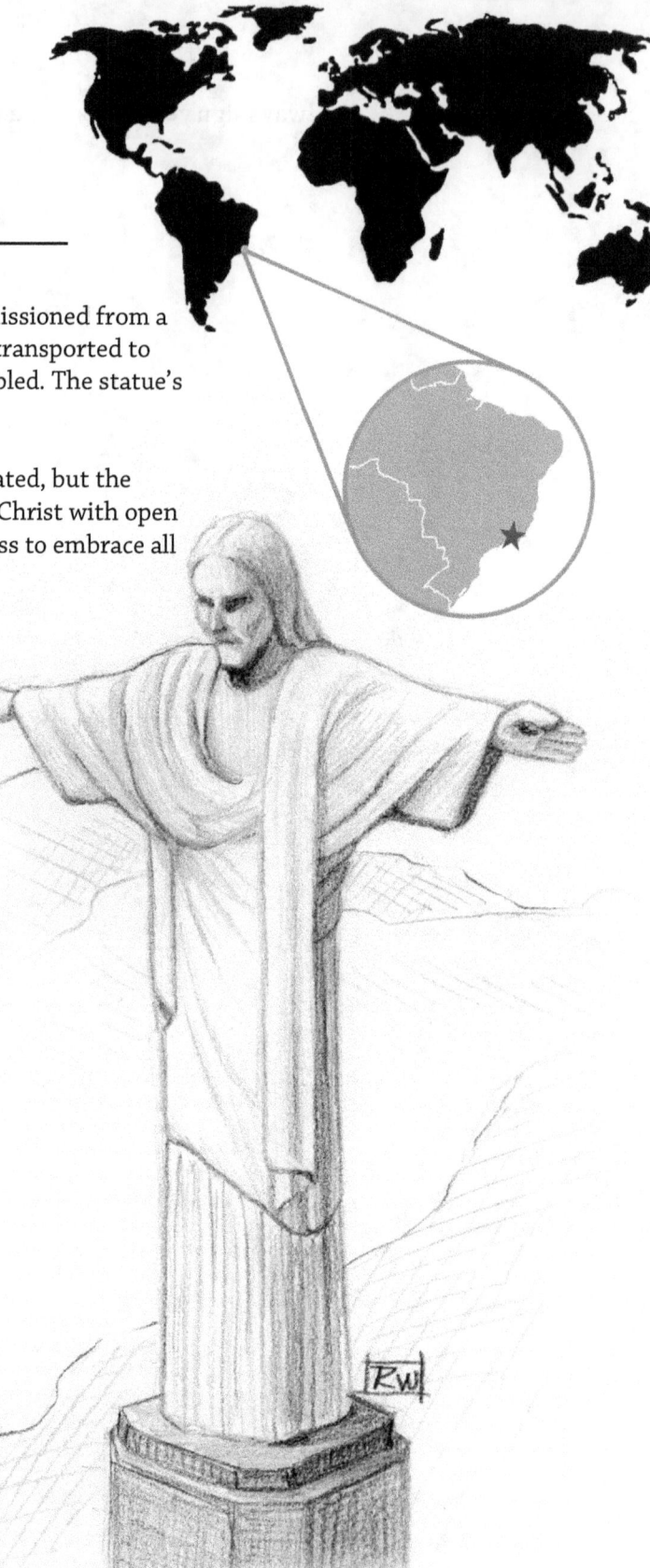

- The statue of Christ the Redeemer was commissioned from a stone quarry in Sweden, built in France, and transported to Rio de Janeiro, Brazil in pieces to be reassembled. The statue's head alone is made up of 50 individual parts.

- Several designs for the statue were contemplated, but the final design was that of a cross-shaped Jesus Christ with open arms, symbolizing Christ's love and willingness to embrace all who come to him.

- The statue is actually more like a mosaic, covered in thousands of small triangular shapes of cut soapstone. These triangles are placed into reinforced concrete to complete the design.

- Replicas and similar statues can be found all over the world; the Philippines, India, the Dominican Republic, Portugal, Italy, Mexico, Peru, Columbia, East Timor, Bolivia, Poland, and Vietnam to name a few.

To sketch fabric, add folds and wrinkles to give a sense of movement.

Chrysler Building

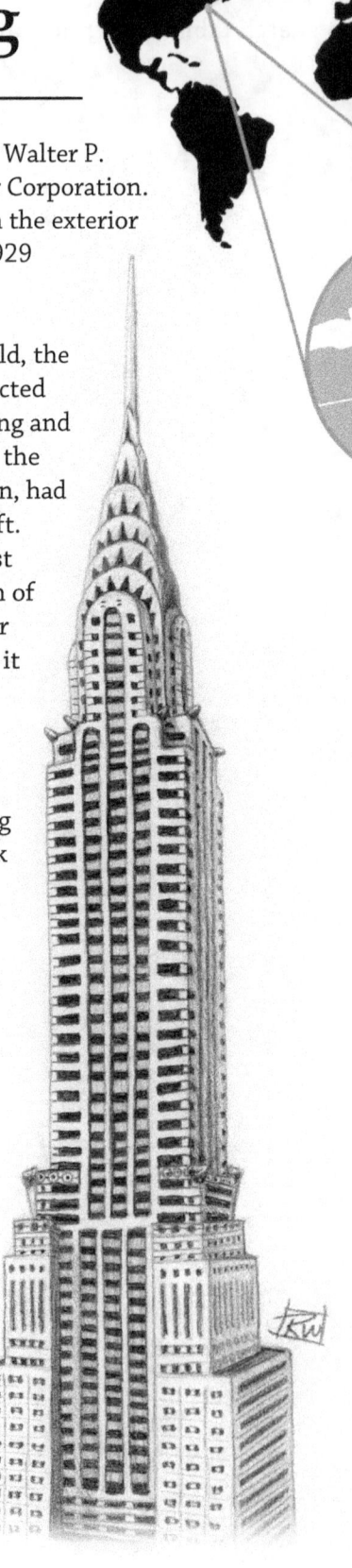

- The Chrysler Building was commissioned by Walter P. Chrysler to be the headquarters for Chrysler Corporation. Therefore, the adornments and gargoyles on the exterior are modeled after the radiator caps of the 1929 Chrysler Plymouth.

- In a race to be the tallest building in the world, the Bank of Manhattan Trust was being constructed around the same time as the Chrysler Building and was designed to be two feet taller. However, the Chrysler Building architect, William Van Alen, had a 125-foot spire secretly built in the fire shaft. The spire topped the Chrysler building in just 90 minutes, only weeks after the completion of the Bank of Manhattan, putting the Chrysler Building at 1,046 feet (319 meters); making it the tallest building in the world at the time.

- In order to complete the Chrysler Building, more than 750 miles of electrical wire was used to construct the skyscraper. This is long enough to cover the distance from New York City to Chicago.

Take your time. If you start feeling frustrated with a drawing, set it aside and take a break. Upon revisiting the sketch, if you are still unhappy, try it again from the beginning.

Church of Our Lady Before Týn

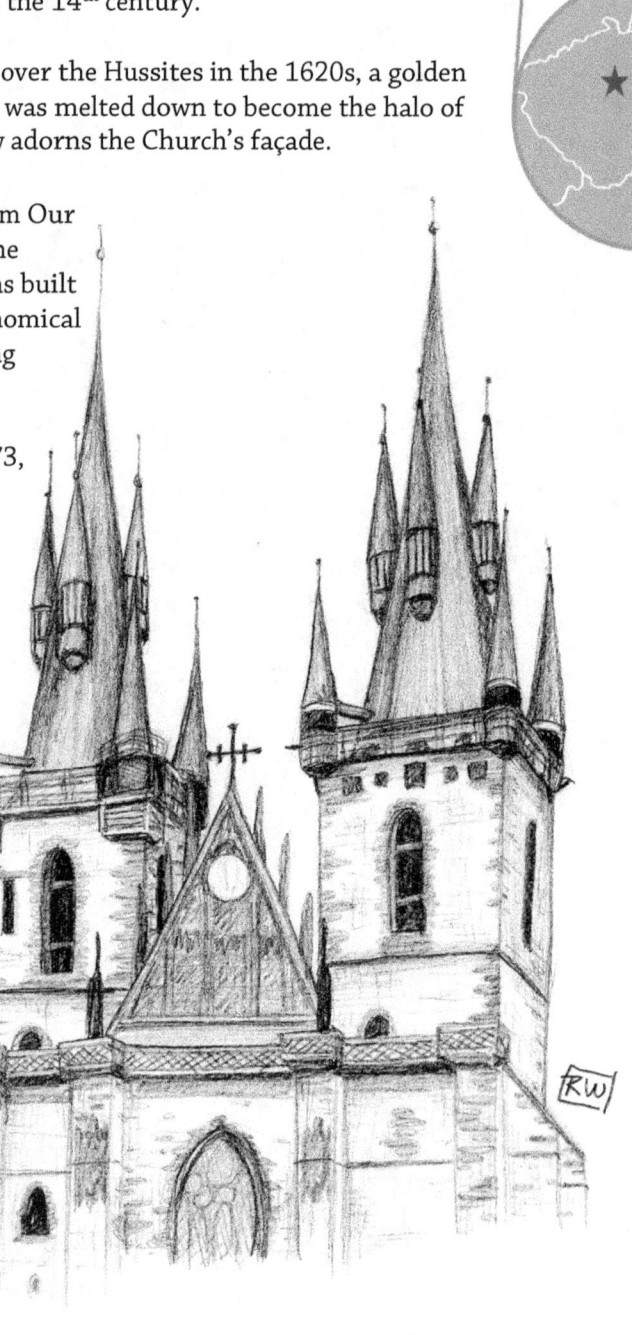

- The Church of Our Lady Before Týn is one of the most important churches in Prague, and has been a dominant part of the Old Town of Prague since the 14th century.

- With the victory of Catholicism over the Hussites in the 1620s, a golden chalice (symbol of the Hussites) was melted down to become the halo of the statue of Madonna that now adorns the Church's façade.

- Across the Old Town Square from Our Lady Before Týn, you can find the Prague astronomical clock. It was built in 1410, and is the oldest astronomical clock in the world still in working order.

- The pipe organ was made in 1673, and is the oldest in Prague.

TIP:

When drawing stones or bricks on a building, no need to cover the whole structure.
Just add accented bricks or stone to avoid overdetailing.

Colosseum

- Originally known as the "Amphitheatrum Flavium", because it was created during the dynasty of Flavian emperors. By the year 1000, the amphitheater took on the name "The Colosseum" due to its proximity to a colossal bronze statue of Nero (which no longer stands today).

- In addition to gladiator spectacles of man vs. beast, the Ancient Romans would flood the Colosseum and host miniature naval battles for entertainment.

- Following damage to the Colosseum from earthquakes and stone robbers, some of the fallen pieces were used to build palaces and churches in Rome, including St. Peter's Basilica in Vatican City.

- In 1948, Italy abolished the death penalty. Since then, the Colosseum became a symbol against capital punishment. Today, should any jurisdiction in the world abolish the death penalty, or if any death sentence is overturned, the lights that illuminate the Colosseum change from white to gold in honor of the event.

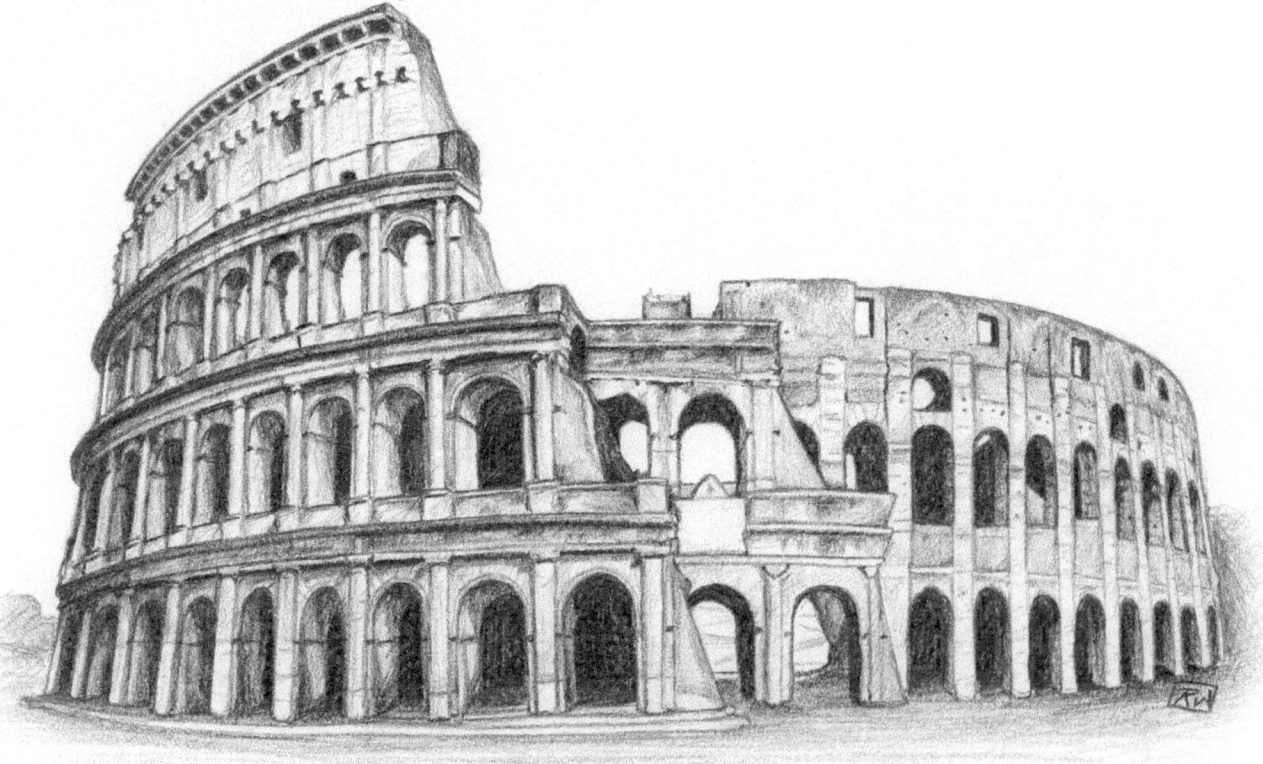

Doorways and windows should always have some shadow, depending on your light source.

Dome of the Rock

- The Dome of the Rock is the oldest surviving Islamic building in the world.

- It is a place of religious blending as well as controversy. The Dome of the Rock is built around the stone location where Muslims believe Muhammad ascended into heaven, as well as the location where the Jews believe Abraham offered his son Isaac as a sacrifice to God. The location of the Dome on Temple Mount is also significant for Christians due to the role of the Temple through the life of Jesus.

- The dome is made of wood that is covered in gold leaf. In 1993, King Hussein of Jordan sold one of his houses in London in order to make a donation of $8.2 million USD to pay for the Dome's gold leaf to be refurbished; 175 pounds (80 kg) of gold was required to complete the job.

- The Dome of the Rock can be found on the back of the 1,000 rial banknote of Iran.

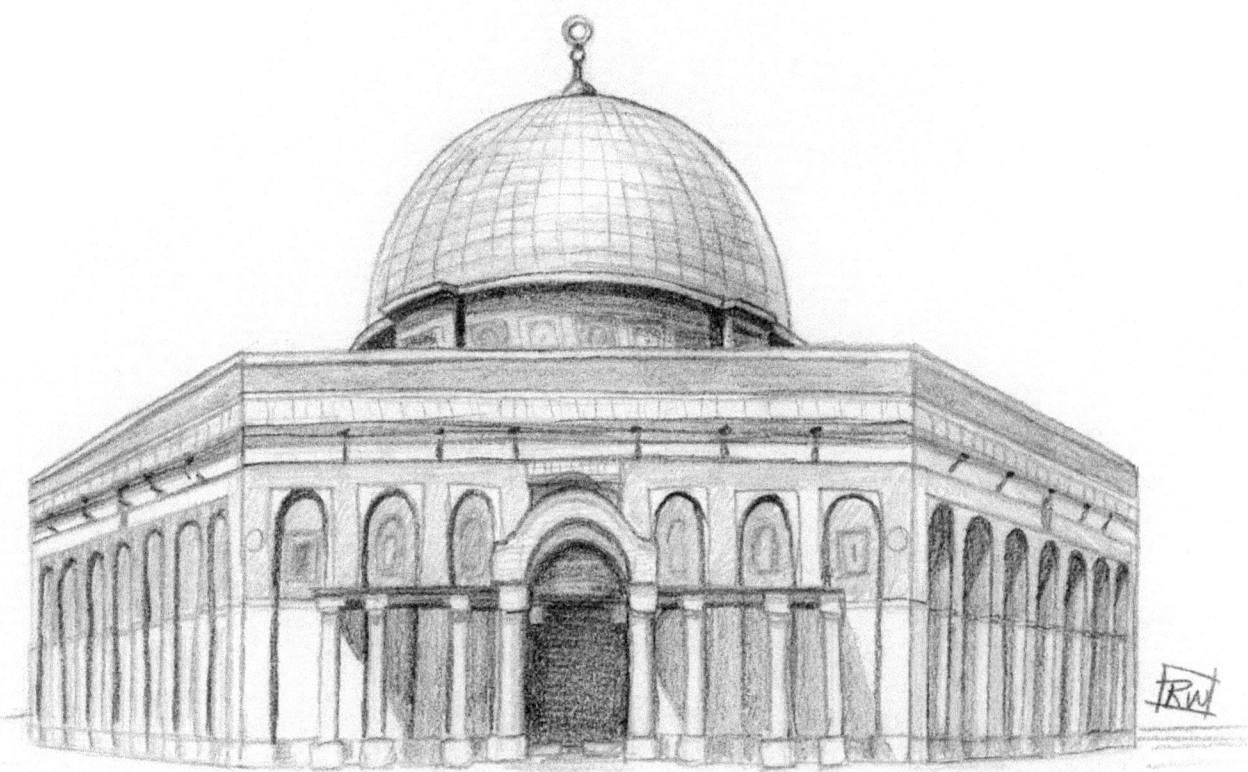

Duomo of Florence

- Florence was the first city in Europe to have paved streets.

- The cathedral took approximately 140 years to build; construction began in September, 1296, and the cathedral was not consecrated until March, 1436.

- Although the cathedral in Florence is commonly known as "Il Duomo," it is not the official name. The structure is officially named Santa Maria del Fiore (Our Lady of the Flower).

- Above the main door inside the cathedral an unusual 24-hour clock can be found. This clock runs on "Italian time"; it has only one hand that runs counter-clockwise and the designated Roman numeral 24 does not represent midnight, but rather the hour of the sunset. The clock is reset on a weekly basis to keep up with the ever-changing hour of sunset.

- The exterior is ornately decorated in tri-color marble panels of pink, green, and white; the interior is considered relatively bare in comparison, apart from the inner dome which is painted with a fresco of the *Last Judgment*.

TIP:
Hard pencils are difficult to draw with.
They leave pale marks, but they are great for light shading.

Eiffel Tower

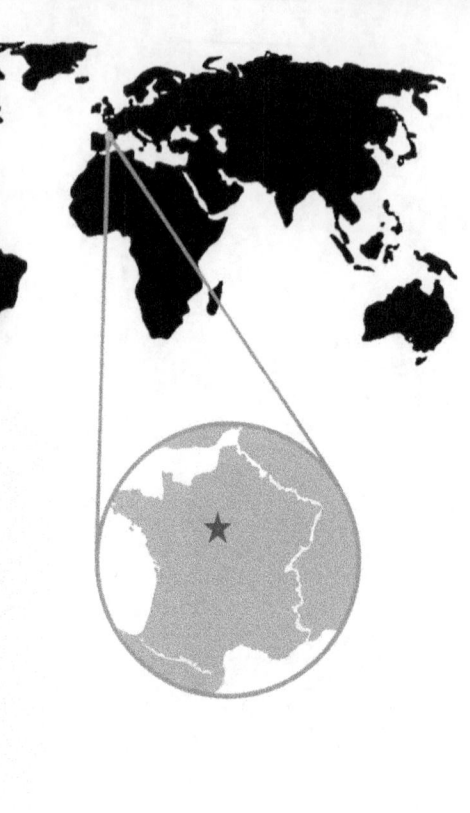

- The Eiffel Tower was originally constructed to serve as the entryway for the World's Fair in 1889.

- Nearly 50 to 60 tons of paint are added to the Eiffel Tower every 7 years to prevent the 10,000 tons of iron from corrosion.

- Temperature can alter the height of the Eiffel Tower. In the summer time, when the tower is exposed to the sun, the tower can be up to six inches (15 cm) taller due to expansion of the building materials.

- The initial lifespan of the tower granted to Gustave Eiffel, was 20 years; it was then to be dismounted and sold as scrap metal. Thankfully this never happened!

- The Eiffel Tower hasn't always been brown. In 1899, the tower was painted yellowish-brown and from 1954 to 1961 it was a reddish-brown, similar to that of the Golden Gate Bridge.

Use a variety of weights in your lines by lifting the pencil or pressing harder.

Empire State Building

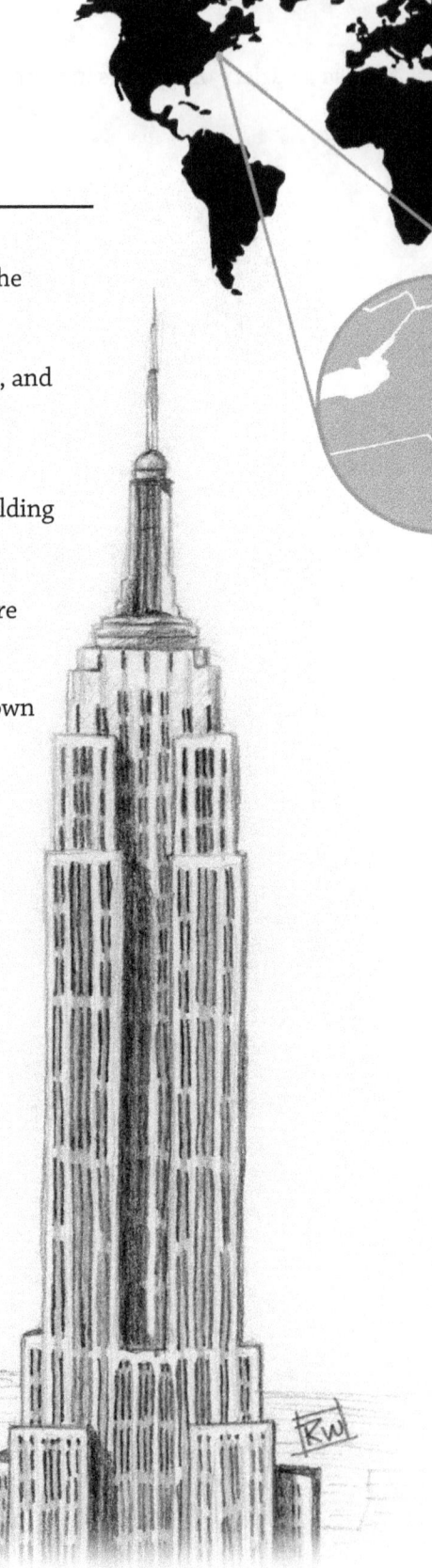

- There are 1,860 steps from street level to the 102nd floor.

- The Empire State Building is 1,454 feet tall, and was the tallest building in the world from 1931-1970.

- The Empire State Building was the first building to have more than 100 floors.

- The building has 6,500 windows, which were remanufactured in 2010 to save energy.

- The Empire State Building is most well-known for the 1933 film, *King Kong*.

- The observation deck made almost $2 million USD its first year!

TIP:

Don't lick your pencil tip.
It is a bad habit that often ruins the mark-making.

Fisherman's Bastion

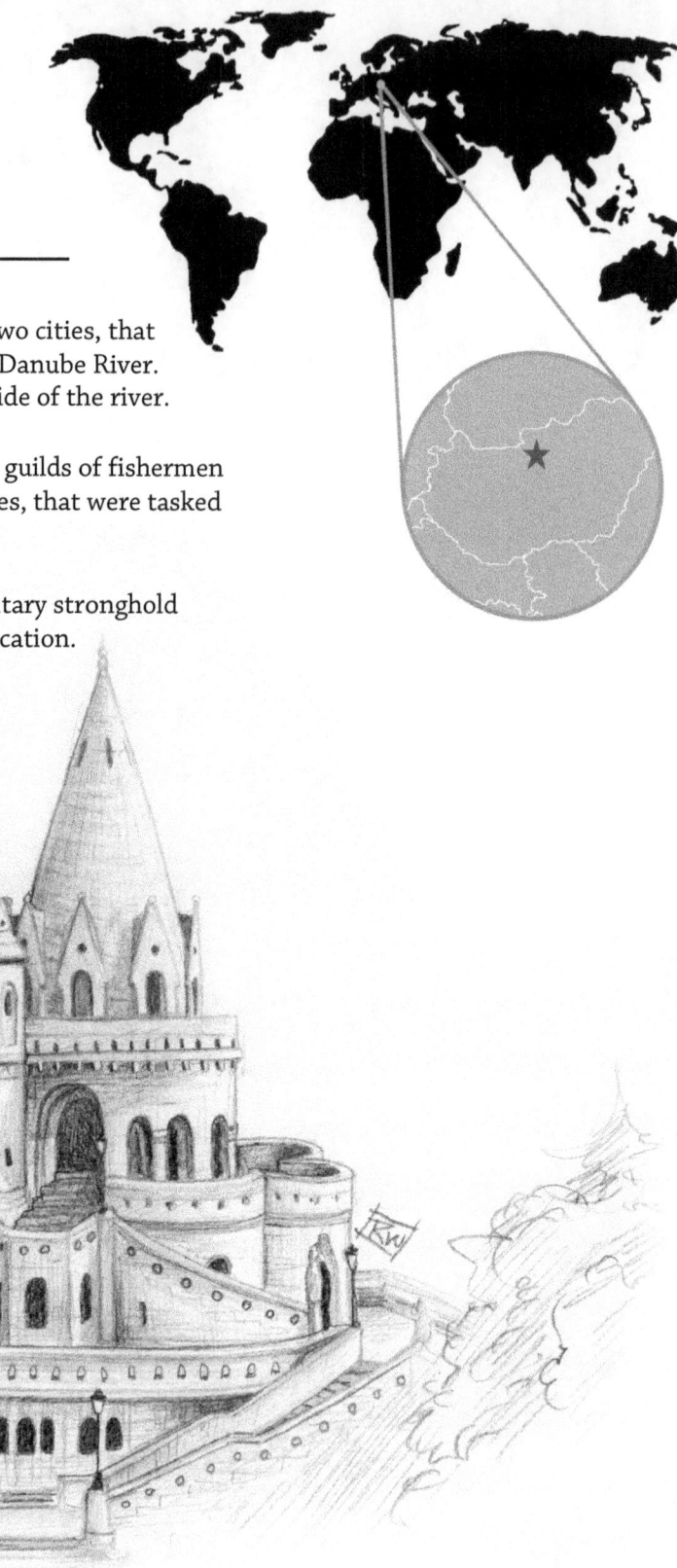

- The city of Budapest is actually divided into two cities, that of Buda and Pest, which are separated by the Danube River. Fisherman's Bastion is actually on the Buda side of the river.

- It is said the structure gets its name from the guilds of fishermen who lived below the bastion in the Middle Ages, that were tasked with protecting the city walls.

- By 1874, the Buda Castle was no longer a military stronghold and, therefore, did not need additional fortification. Fisherman's Bastion then served as a viewing terrace for beautiful panoramic views of the Danube River and the city of Pest on the opposite bank.

- The seven turrets of the bastion symbolize the seven Hungarian chieftains who led their tribes to settle in Hungary in 896 AD.

You can sharpen your pencil tips with a scalpel rather than a sharpener tool. It takes slightly longer, but it gives you more control over the shape of the pencil point.

Gateway Arch of St. Louis

- Construction began on the Arch on Februrary 12th, 1963 and was completed on October 28th, 1965.

- There are 32 windows in the top of the Arch.

- At its base, each leg of the Arch is 54 feet (16.5 meters) wide, where at the top the dimension is 17 feet (5.2 meters) in width.

- The Arch is 63 stories tall, each story measuring 10 feet.

- The Arch was designed to sway as much as 18 inches. However, under normal conditions, the Arch does not sway. It takes 50 mph (80km/h) winds to shift the top 1.5 inches either side of the center.

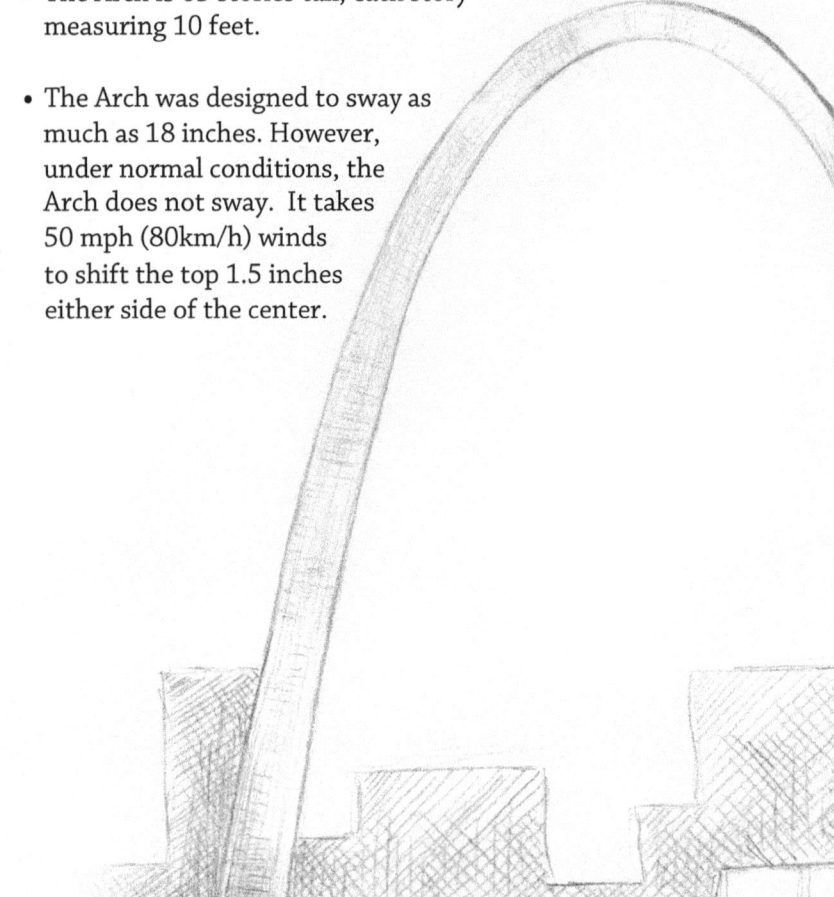

Draw on the kind of paper that works well in collaboration with your pencils. Test on the surfaces to see if they're too smooth or rough.

Giant's Causeway

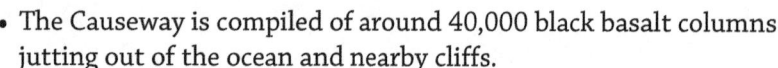

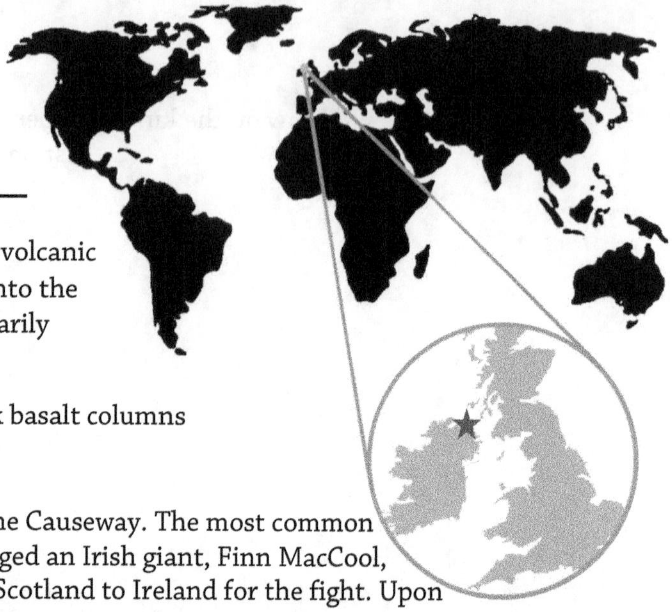

- The Giant's Causeway was formed due to ancient volcanic activity. Lava welling up through fissures oozed into the ocean and cooled, forming columns that are primarily hexagonal in shape.

- The Causeway is compiled of around 40,000 black basalt columns jutting out of the ocean and nearby cliffs.

- There are various myths around the creation of the Causeway. The most common being a Scottish giant, Benandonner, who challenged an Irish giant, Finn MacCool, to a fight. The Scottish giant, built a bridge from Scotland to Ireland for the fight. Upon arrival, Finn MacCool's wife disguised Finn as a baby and put him in a cradle and said his father wasn't home. When Benandonner saw the size of MacCool's "baby", he feared the size of MacCool himself, and went running back to Scotland, destroying the bridge behind him. This could be influenced by the fact that a similar rock formation exists off the coast of the Scottish Isle of Staffa.

- A number of rare plant species have also been found on cliffs near the Giant's Causeway, such as vernal squill, frog orchid, hare's foot trefoil, sea spleenwort and sea fescue; it sounds like an ingredient list from a mythical cookbook!

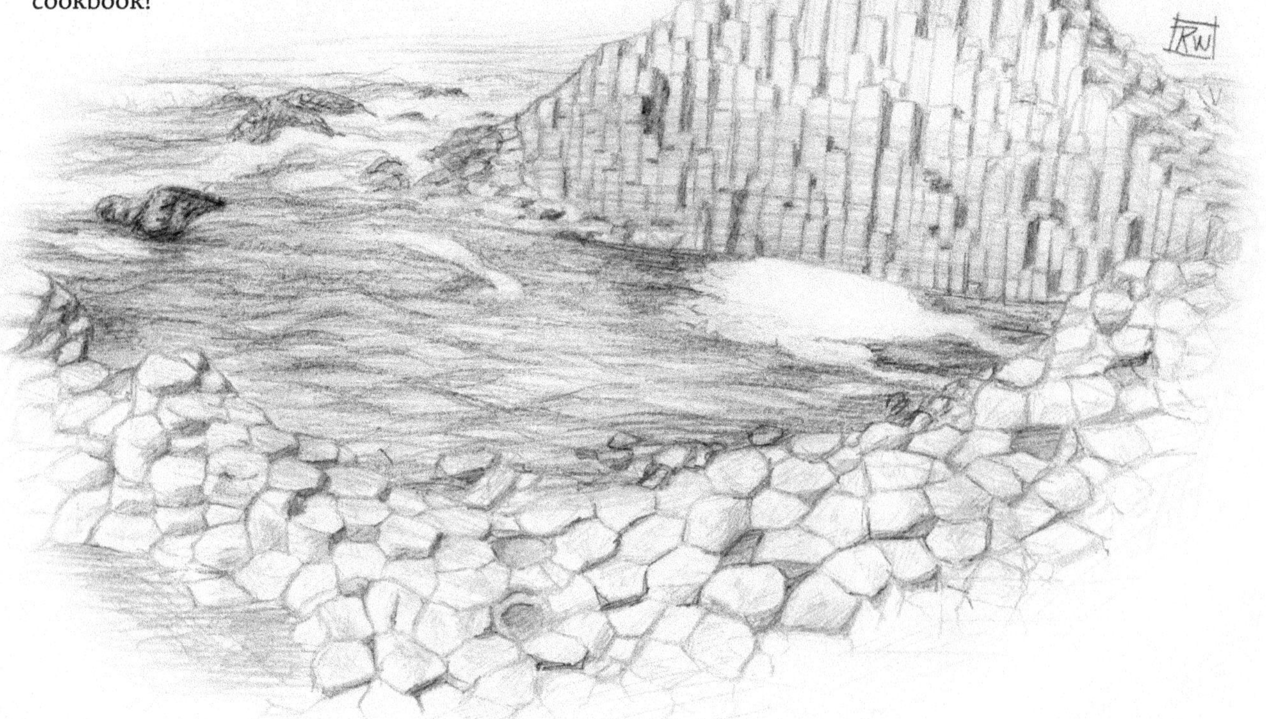

La Giralda

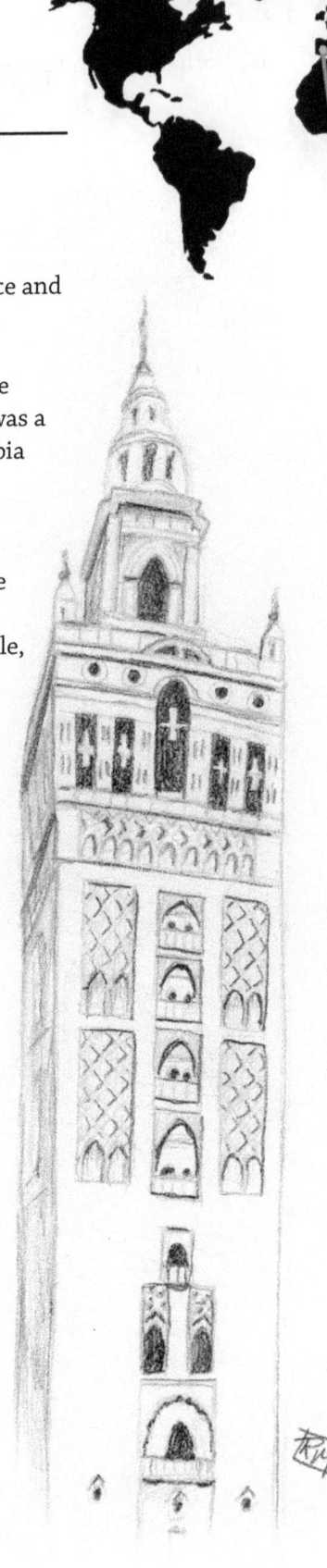

- The Cathedral of Seville, is the largest Gothic cathedral in the world.

- The cathedral is home to the final resting place and the tomb of Christopher Columbus.

- The Giralda Tower is now the bell tower of the Cathedral of Seville. However, historically it was a minaret for a mosque, modeled from Koutoubia Mosque in Marrakech, Morocco.

- There is a replica of La Giralda tower that is half of the original tower's size, located on the Country Club Plaza in Kansas City, Missouri. The tower was added here in 1967 when Seville, Spain and Kansas City became sister cities.

Giza Necropolis

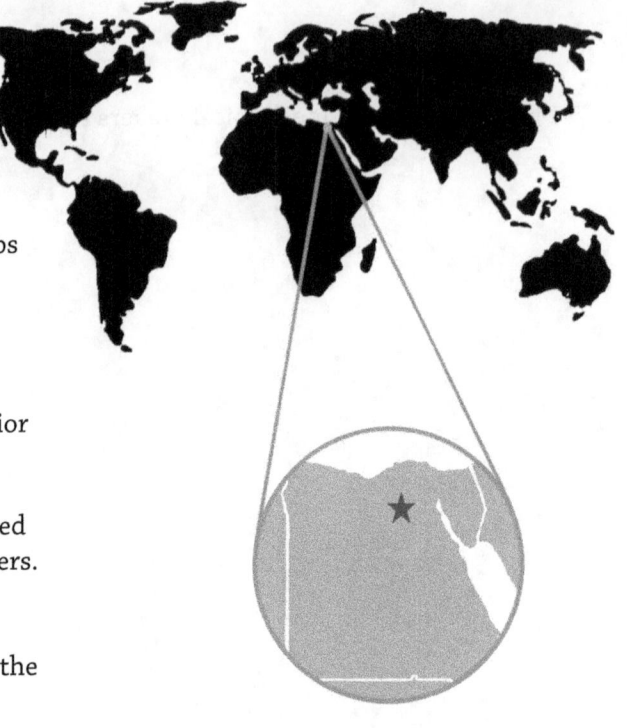

- Most pyramids are built as burial monuments or tombs for the Egyptian pharaohs.

- Almost all Egyptian pyramids are located on the west bank of the Nile, as this is the side of the setting sun where the soul of the deceased would meet the sun prior to its descent.

- Construction of the Great Pyramids of Giza is estimated at about 23 years, with a team of around 25,000 workers.

- The pyramid shape was said to have been chosen to honor the Egyptian sun god, Ra, the ruler of creation; the shape is believed to symbolize the rays of the sun.

- The interior temperature of the pyramids is that of the earth, remaining constantly at 68° F (20° C).

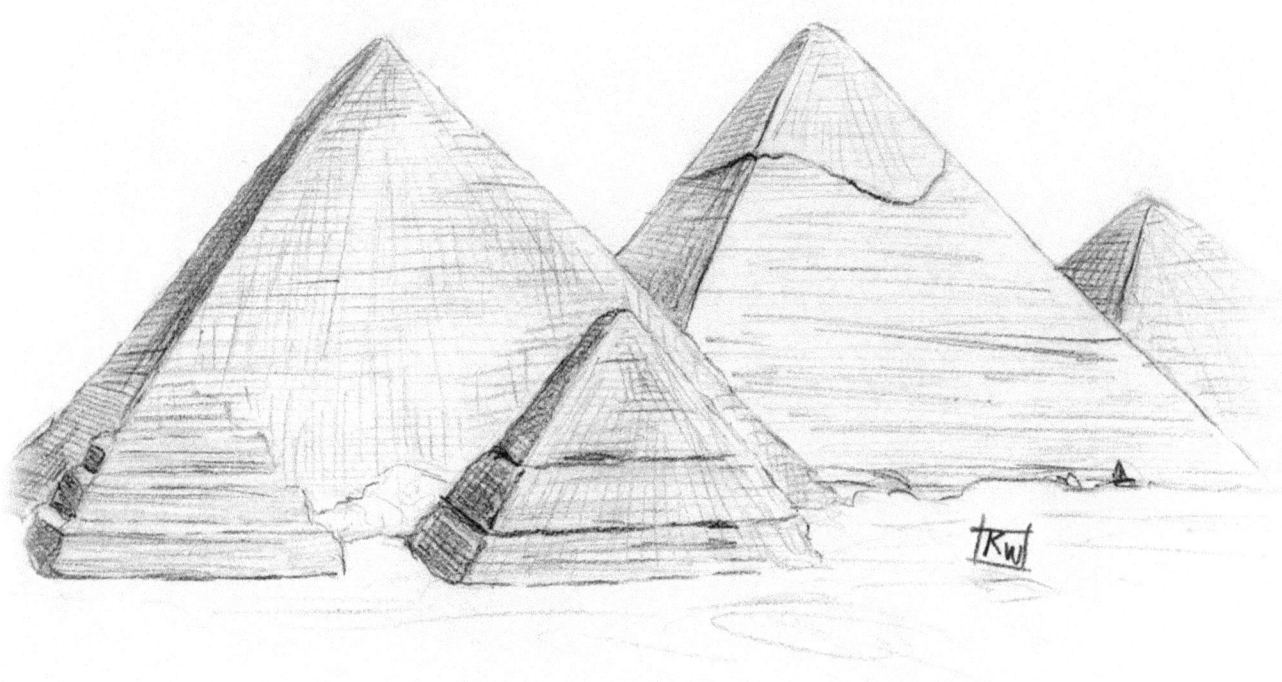

Golden Gate Bridge

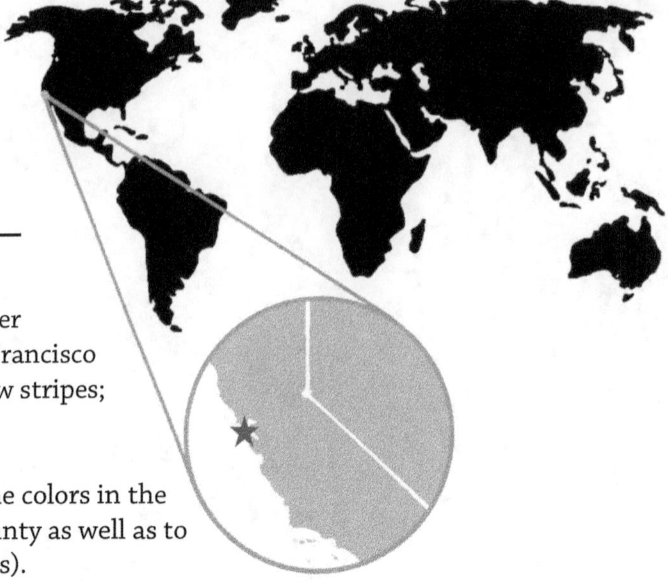

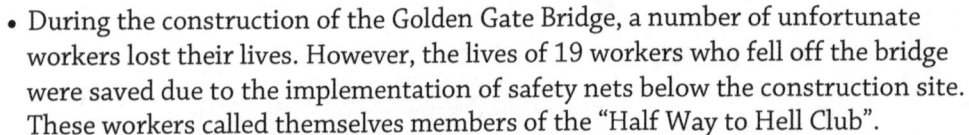

- The U.S. Navy was concerned that fog would hinder visibility of the bridge for ships coming into San Francisco Bay and requested it be painted in black and yellow stripes; thankfully, this wasn't allowed!

- The paint chosen for the bridge was to enhance the colors in the natural landscape of the nearby hills in Marin County as well as to increase visibility in fog (without the garish stripes).

- During the construction of the Golden Gate Bridge, a number of unfortunate workers lost their lives. However, the lives of 19 workers who fell off the bridge were saved due to the implementation of safety nets below the construction site. These workers called themselves members of the "Half Way to Hell Club".

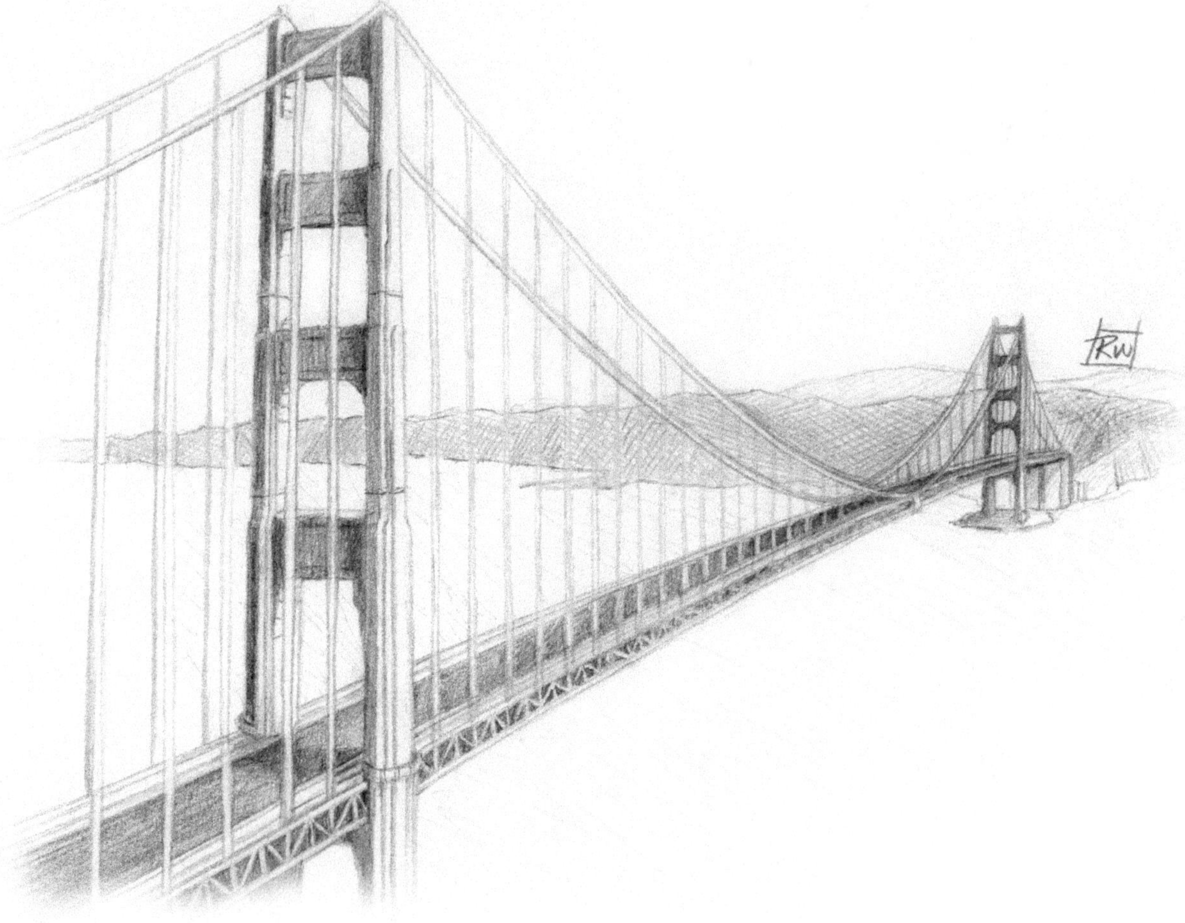

Feel free to use a ruler to achieve straight lines; don't worry, it's not cheating!

Grand Canyon

- The rim of the Grand Canyon is not exactly even; the North Rim stands at 7,800 feet (2,377 meters) deep, where the South Rim is at 2,400 feet (731 meters) deep.

- The Colorado River cuts through the canyon through a layer of rock that is 1.75 billion years old!

- Around 800 million gallons (3,028 million liters) of water per hour flow through the canyon via the Colorado River.

- In 1956, two eastbound commercial planes were flying from Los Angeles to Chicago. Both flew over the Grand Canyon (unmonitored airspace) for a better view, and ultimately ended in a mid-air collision where 128 people perished. This incident prompted the creation of the independent body of the Federal Aviation Agency (FAA), later known as the Federal Aviation Administration, to oversee safety in the airline industry.

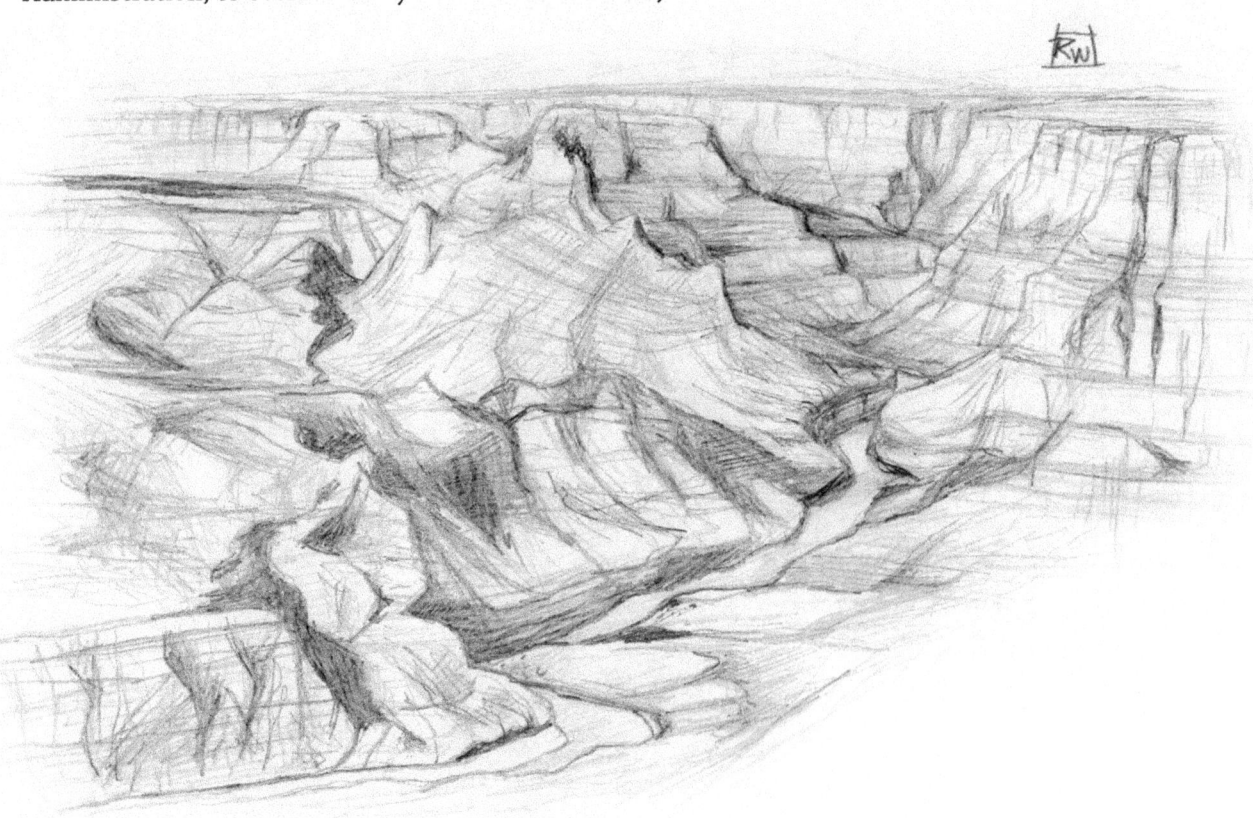

TIP:
Use softer rubber erasers to wipe away outlines or mistakes.
Hard rubber essentially rips off the top layer of the paper.

Great Buddha of Kōtoku-in

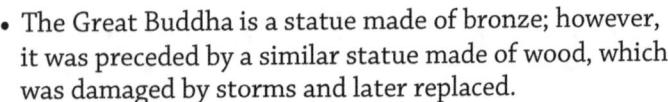

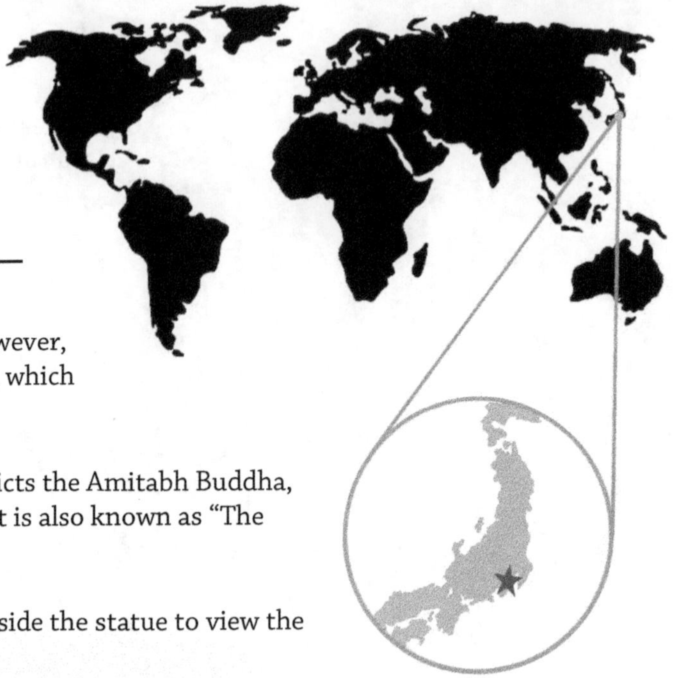

- The Great Buddha is a statue made of bronze; however, it was preceded by a similar statue made of wood, which was damaged by storms and later replaced.

- The statue is in the seated lotus position and depicts the Amitabh Buddha, which is one of the most famous icons of Japan; it is also known as "The Buddha of Infinite Light".

- The statue is hollow, so visitors can actually go inside the statue to view the interior and see how it was constructed.

- Over the centuries, the statue was housed inside of a hall structure. However, due to storms and a tsunami in the 15th century, the housing was washed away and since then, the Buddha now stands in open air.

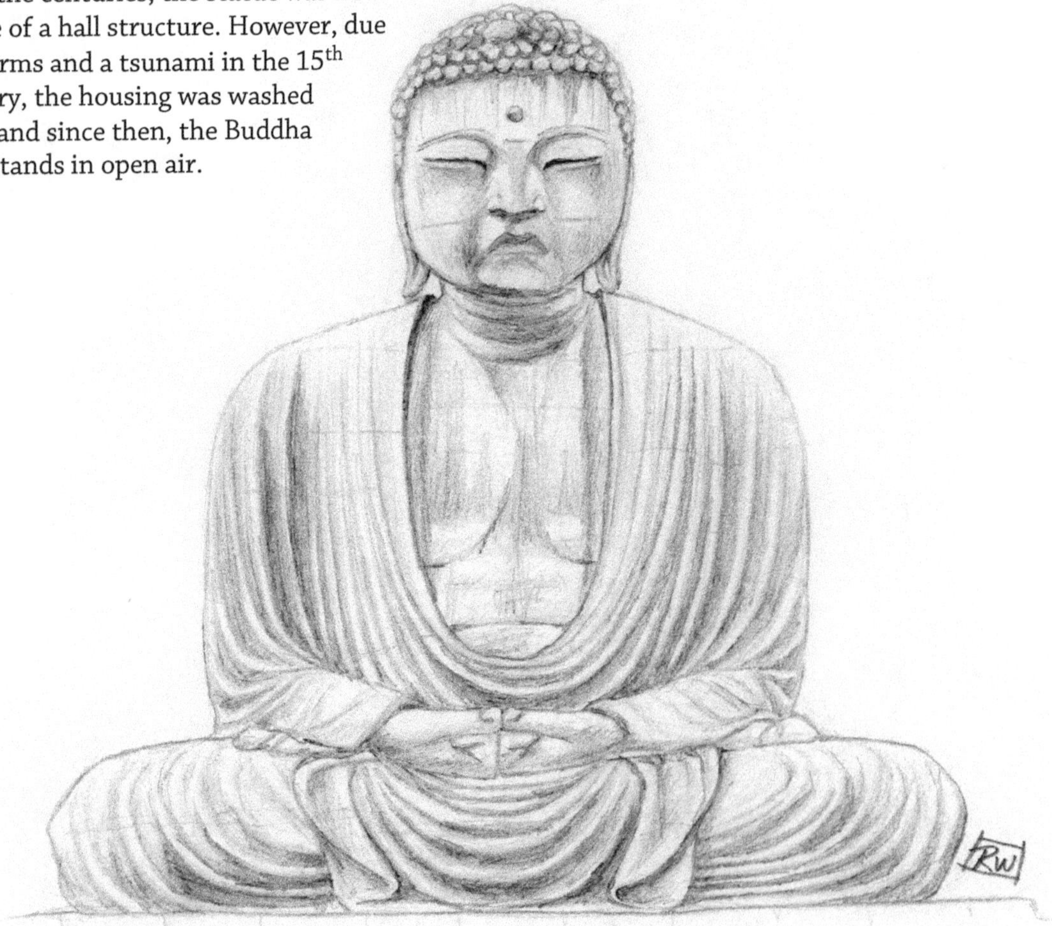

A high contrast of light and dark shades gives the drawing a sense of real depth.

Great Mosque of Cordoba

- The Great Mosque, or Mezquita, of Cordoba is a unique architectural oddity symbolizing the religious changes in Cordoba over the centuries. It is an all-encompassing building where the major religions of Islam and Christianity share a common place in history.

- In 784 AD, the mosque was built on the same site as a Visigoth church from 500 AD. Today, there is a hole in the floor allowing for the viewing of the original Visigothic remains.

- Although the mosque has been consecrated as a Catholic church since 1236, since the year 2000, Muslims have lobbied for rights to pray in the Mezquita and have even lodged a formal request with the Vatican.

- The harmonious continuity of the 856 soaring arches inside the Mezquita is even continued into the courtyard, where rows of orange trees are planted in a uniform manner to mirror with the interior's methodical arrangement.

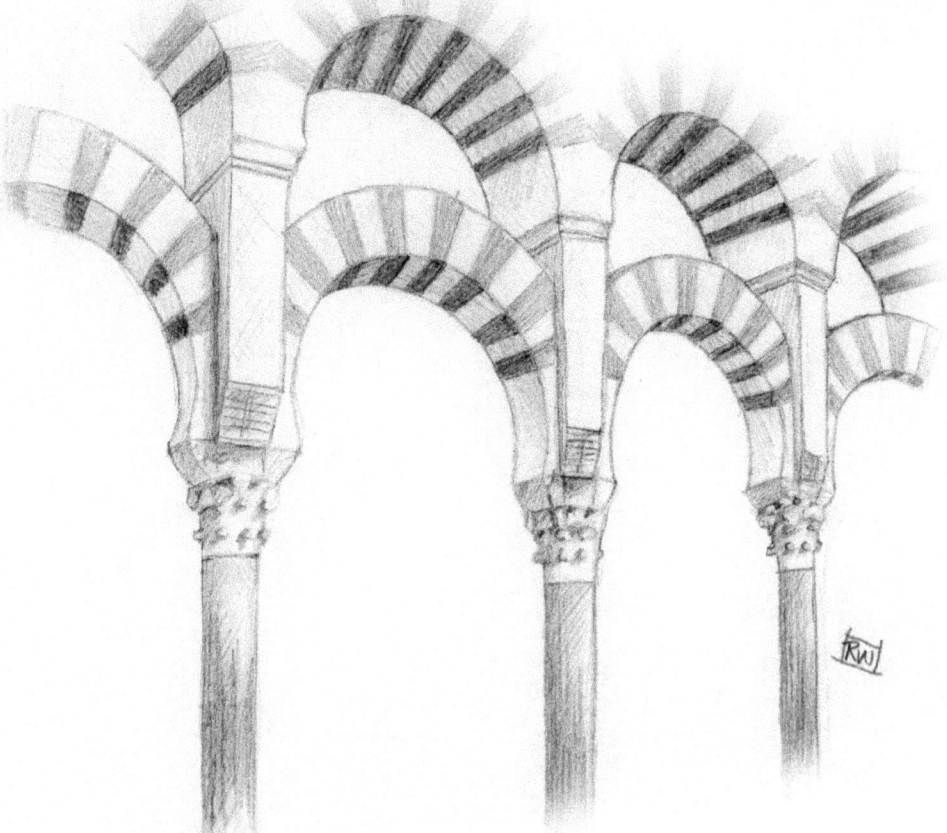

TIP:

Don't be afraid to shade black in the darkest parts or leave the lightest parts untouched.

Great Sphinx of Giza

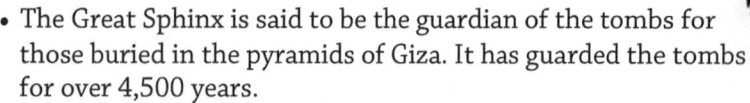

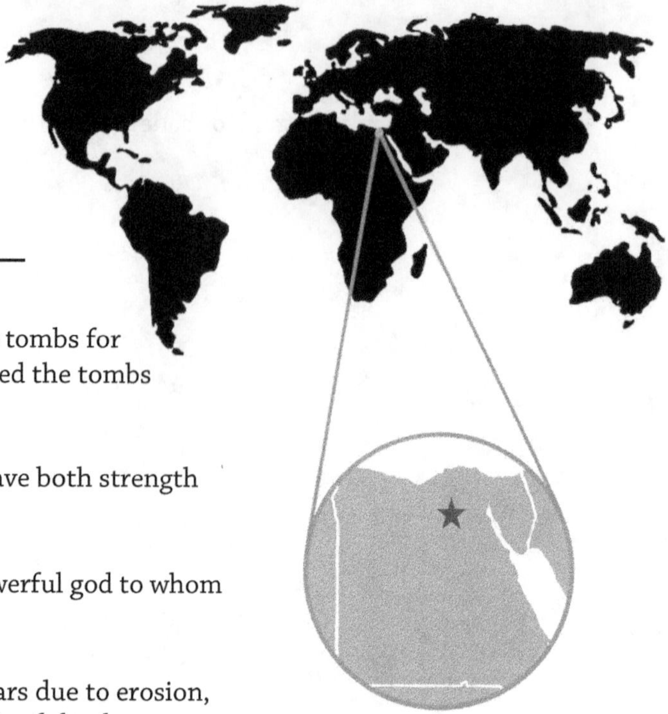

- The Great Sphinx is said to be the guardian of the tombs for those buried in the pyramids of Giza. It has guarded the tombs for over 4,500 years.

- The Sphinx is part human, part lion; it's said to have both strength and knowledge.

- Ancient Egyptians believed the Sphinx to be a powerful god to whom they worshipped and offered sacrifices.

- The Sphinx has been greatly damaged over the years due to erosion, pollution from nearby Cairo and the blowing sands of the desert.

- The body and head of the Sphinx are carved out of limestone found on site, and the paws were added later out of separate pieces of stone.

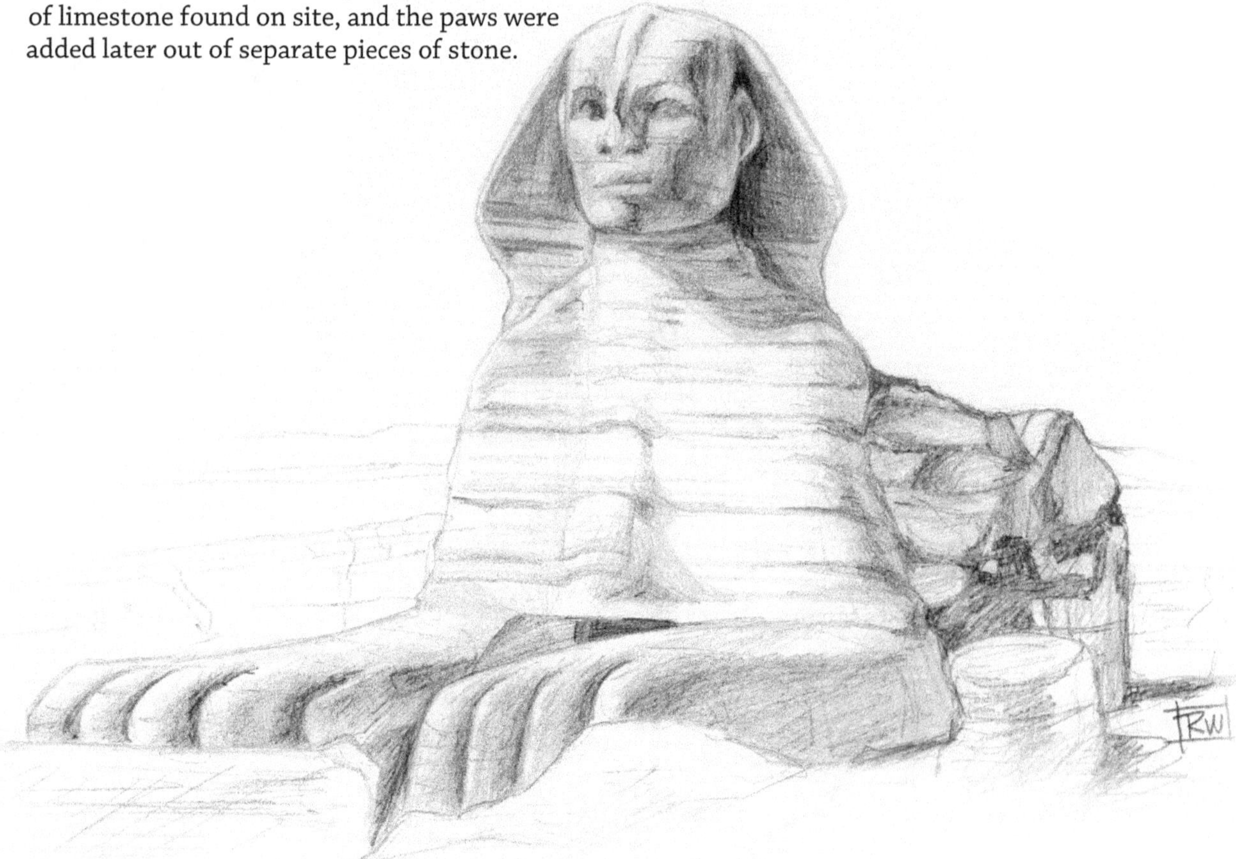

Test your eraser on a blank piece of paper to check that it's clean and won't leave behind streaks.

Great Wall of China

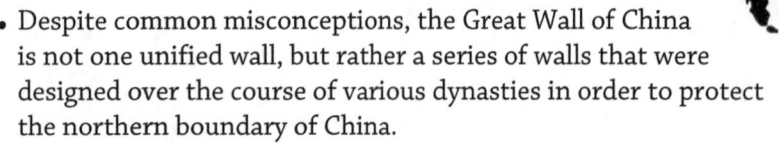

- Despite common misconceptions, the Great Wall of China is not one unified wall, but rather a series of walls that were designed over the course of various dynasties in order to protect the northern boundary of China.

- Even though the wall was built to protect China from invaders, it didn't really serve its purpose. In 1211 and 1223 AD, Genghis Khan, leader of the Mongols, easily went around the wall in places where it was not joined and proceeded to conquer northern China.

- Contrary to myths, the mortar to build the Great Wall was made from rice flour and not the bones of humans who died during construction of the wall.

- The Great Wall of China is the longest man-made structure in the world, but is not visible from space, as some would believe.

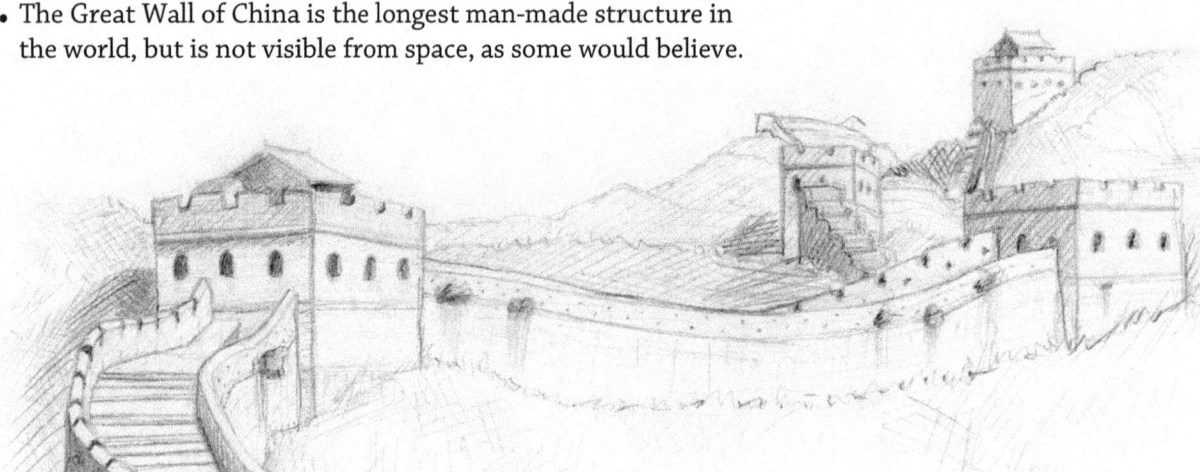

TIP:

Don't feel like you have to detail every aspect of your sketch. Focus on the main subject matter and leave the background plain.

Halong Bay

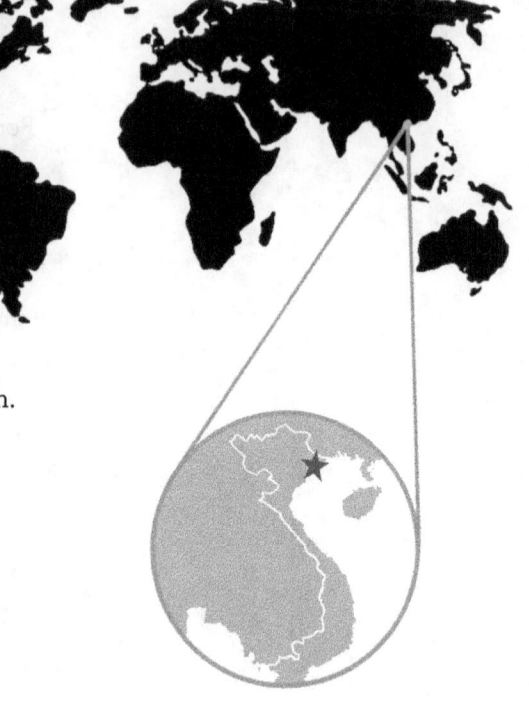

- A legend exists recounting the creation of Halong Bay. It's said that Vietnam was trying to protect itself from invaders, so the gods sent dragons to protect the country. These dragons spit out jewels that fell into the sea, forming islands, mountains, and rocks. Then, as enemies attacked, their boats would run ashore and wreck on the islands, protecting Vietnam.

- In reality, the bay has formed over 500 million years with the limestone rocks wearing away due to tropical, moist climate in the region.

- There are over 2,000 islands that make up Halong Bay.

- Over half of the islands have not been named. With severely steep edges and staggering heights, many of the islands are dangerous to explore and remain largely untouched.

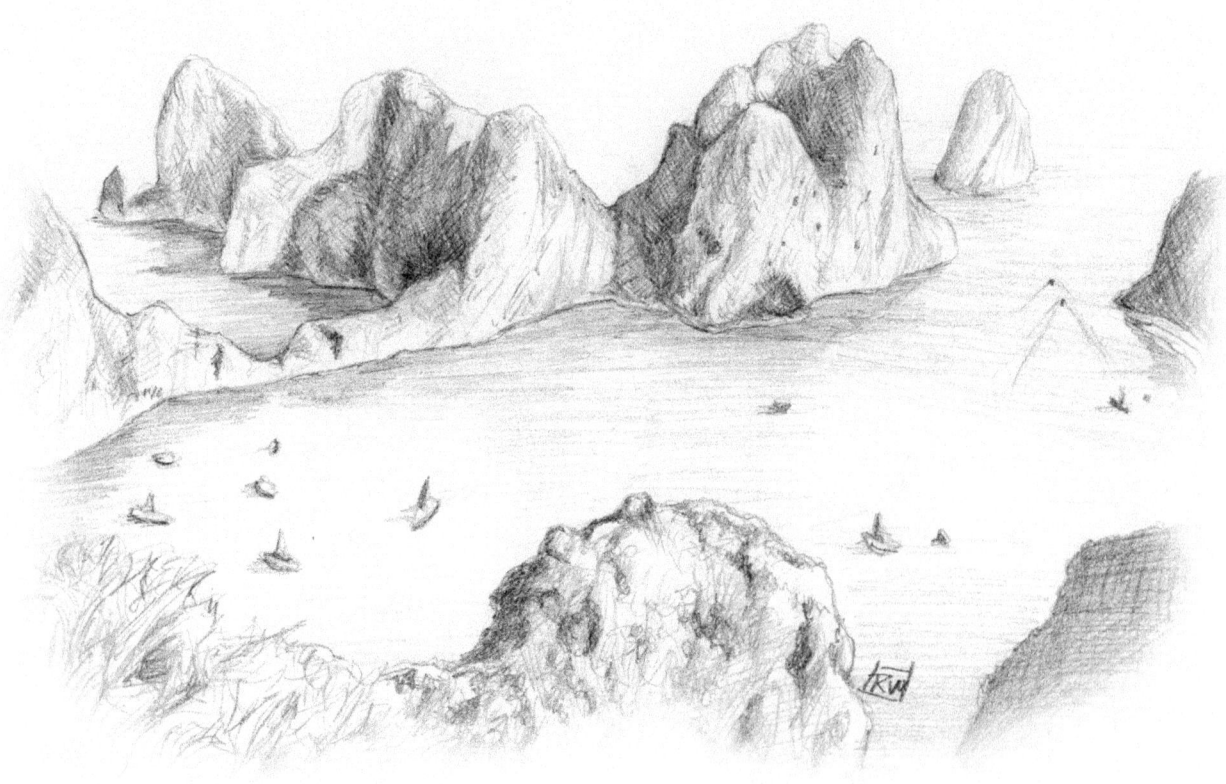

Hills of Tuscany

- The origin of the Italian language was developed in Tuscany. Literary works from authors such as Dante Alighieri were widely read throughout Italy. Dante's written dialect became the model for educated Italians, therefore, standardizing the official Italian language.

- Although *Pinocchio* may be a well-known Disney animated film, the true character originated in Tuscany. In 1883, Carlo Collodi wrote *The Adventures of Pinocchio*, based on the story of a wooden marionette that comes to life.

- The Via Chiantigiana is one of the most beautiful roads across all of the Italian landscapes. The road winds through the vineyards, towns, villages, and Chianti wine zone, connecting Florence to Siena.

- From the previous fact you may have guessed, the full-bodied red wine known as Chianti originated in Tuscany in the Chianti Mountains.

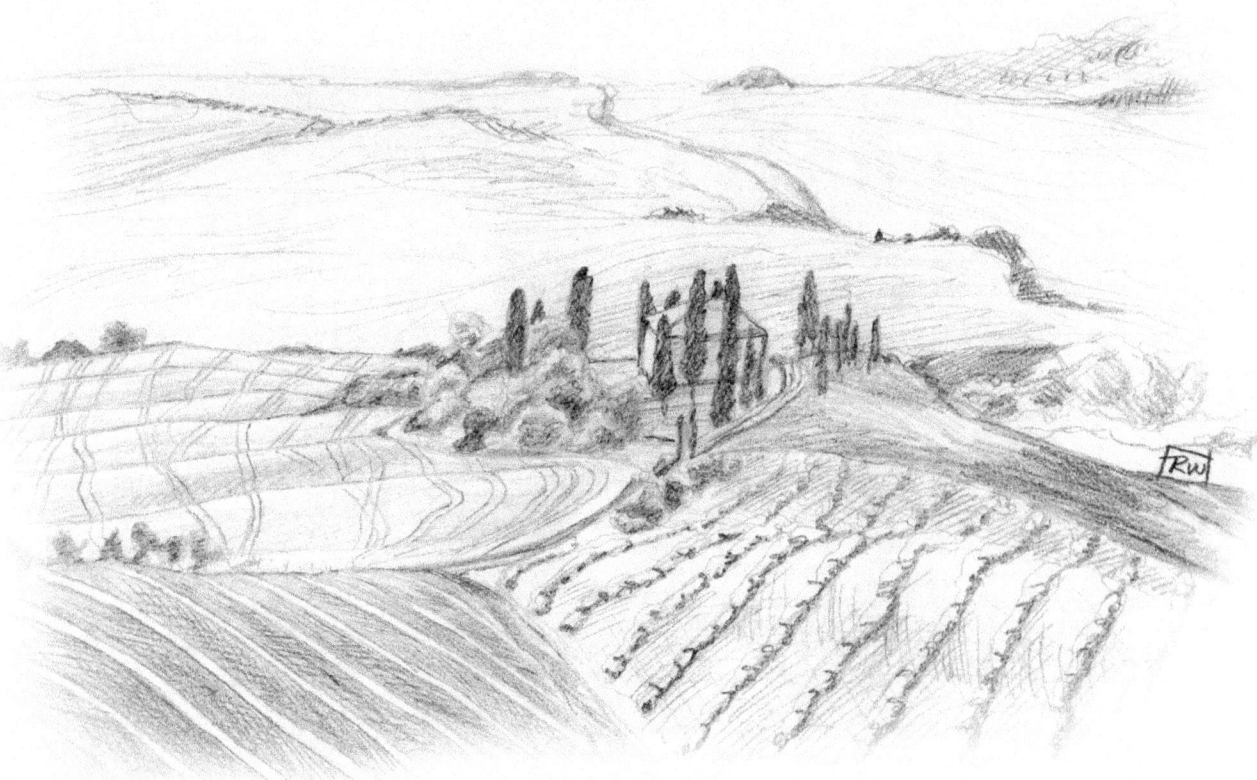

Detail is important when showing a sense of space.
Objects closer to the viewer should have crisper detail than objects further away.

Imperial Palace, Forbidden City

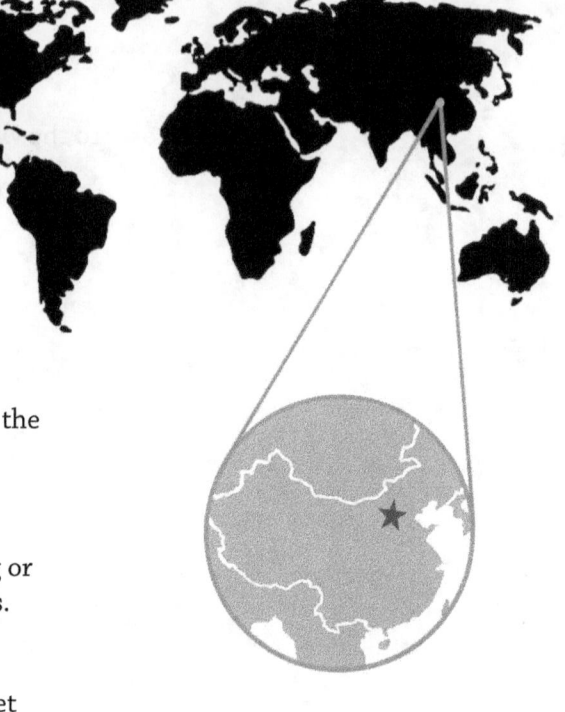

- The Forbidden City has been home to 24 emperors: 10 from the Qing dynasty and 14 from the Ming dynasty.

- The term "forbidden" comes from the fact that one needed the emperor's permission to enter or leave the palace.

- The city is made up of 980 buildings, housing 9,999 rooms which are ornately decorated with statues. As each building or room grows in importance, the number of statues increases. The most important room has at least ten statues.

- The Forbidden City is contained by a wall that stands 26 feet (8 meters) high, as well as a moat that is 20 feet (6 meters) deep.

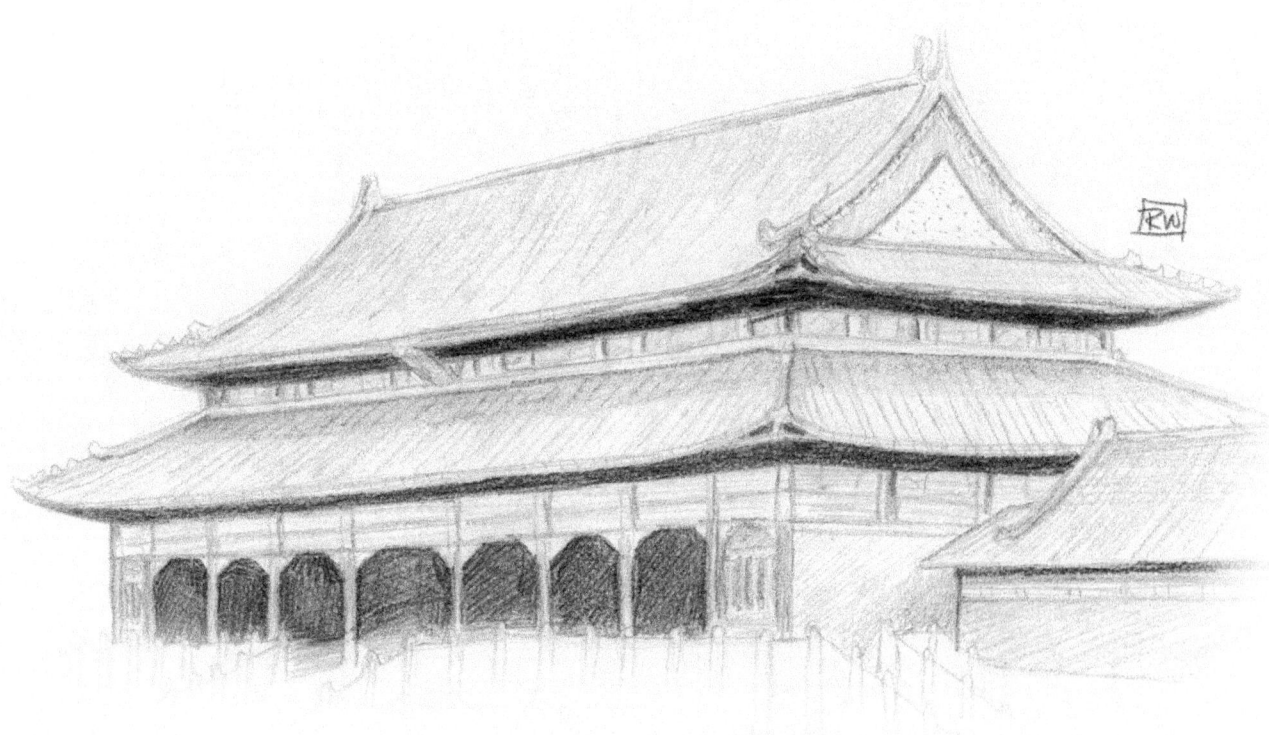

Kangaroo at
Ayers Rock

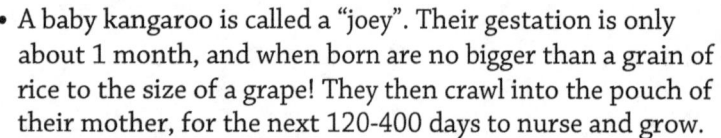

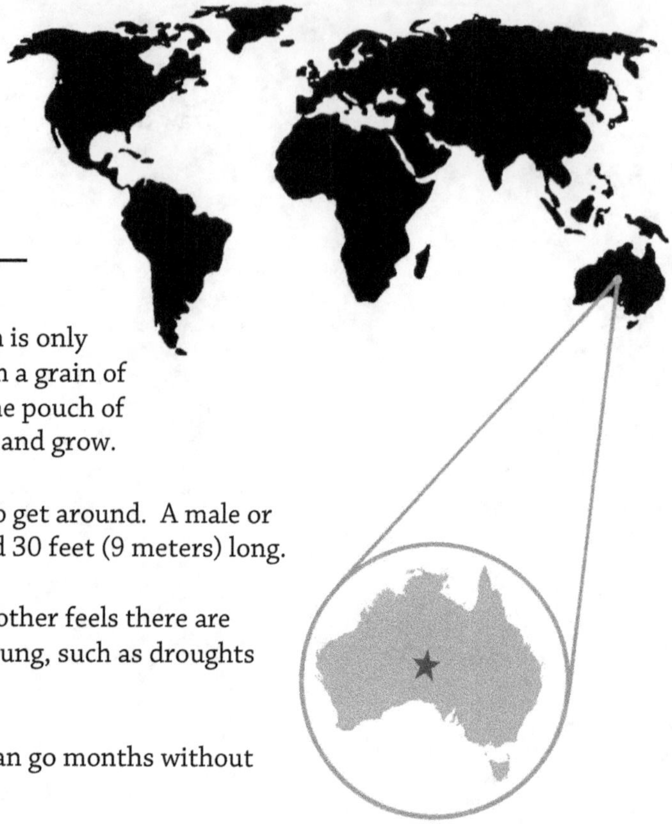

- A baby kangaroo is called a "joey". Their gestation is only about 1 month, and when born are no bigger than a grain of rice to the size of a grape! They then crawl into the pouch of their mother, for the next 120-400 days to nurse and grow.

- Kangaroos use hopping as their primary means to get around. A male or "buck" can jump up to 10 feet (3 meters) high and 30 feet (9 meters) long.

- Female kangaroos can prolong gestation if the mother feels there are factors that would threaten the survival of her young, such as droughts or lack of food sources.

- Kangaroos need very little water to survive and can go months without drinking if necessary.

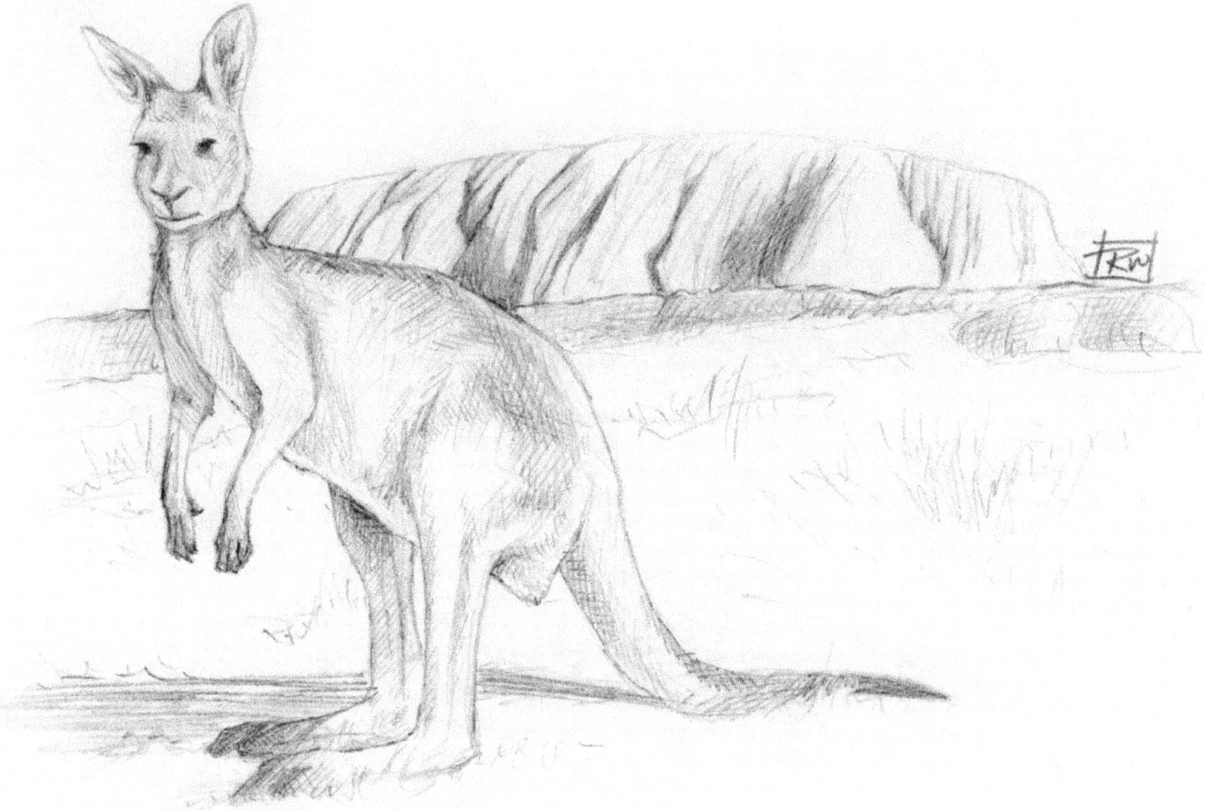

TIP:
Sketching animals is different in every sense.
Use cross-hatch shading for a more layered appearance of form; it's also quicker.

Kraków

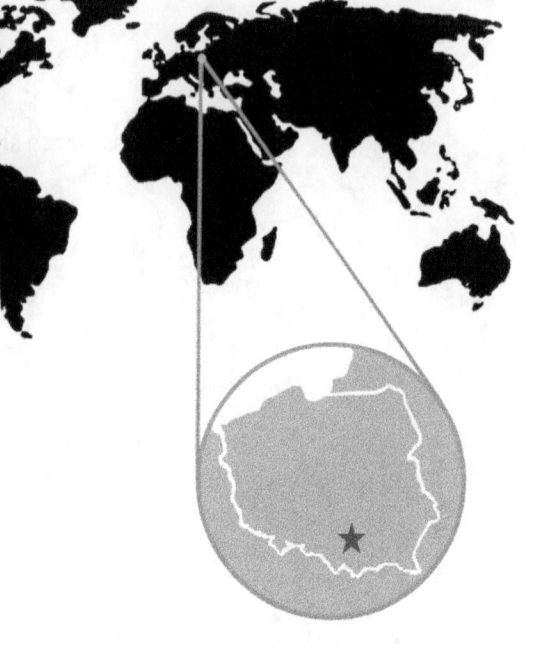

- Kraków was the capital of Poland from 1038 - 1596.

- There is a legend that Kraków's name is derived from a ruler named Krakus, who built the town over a cave that was home to a ravenous dragon. Krakus vanquished the dragon by feeding it poisonous lamb and from then on the city was free.

- Kraków is home to the largest medieval market square in all of Europe. It is known as, the Rynek Główny and is over 430,000 ft^2 (40,000 m^2).

- Kraków is a city bursting with culture and education. It is home to more than 24 establishments of higher education, 6,000 historical sites, and more than two million works of art.

TIP:

Sketching details lightly such as buildings in the background, gives the illusion of distance.

Leaning Tower of Pisa

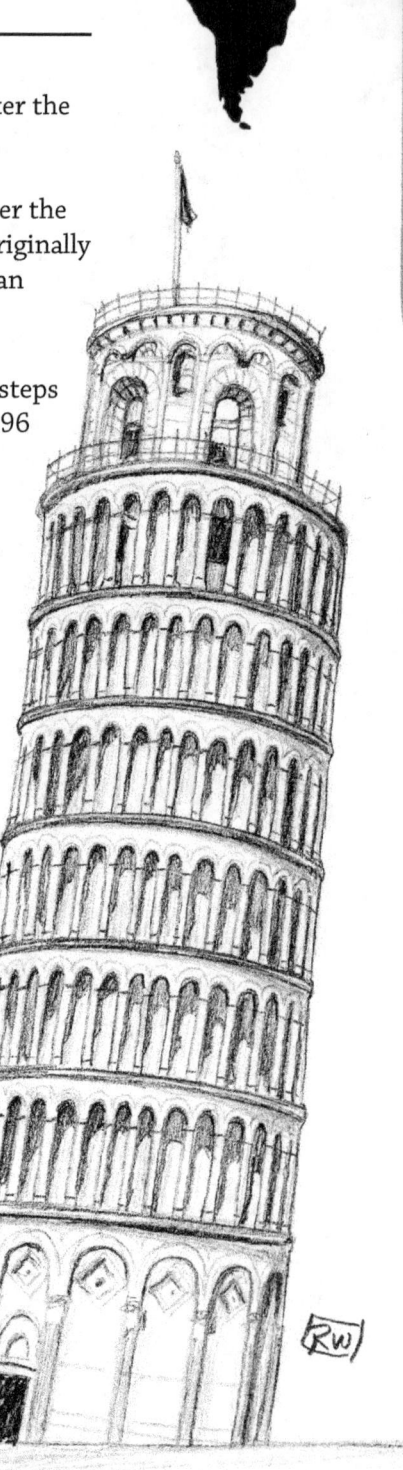

- The tower began to lean early on; shortly after the construction of the second story.

- The lean of the tower has been decreased over the years with several restorations. The tower originally sat at a 5.5 degree lean and today sits at a lean of 3.97 degrees.

- To account for the lean, there are two more steps on the south of the tower, than the north (296 steps on the south, 294 steps on the north).

- During World War II, the Germans used the tower as a lookout point. The Allies knew this, but would not bomb the tower due to its beauty.

TIP:

Use light sketch lines for construction, helping to align windows or columns with each other.

Louvre Museum

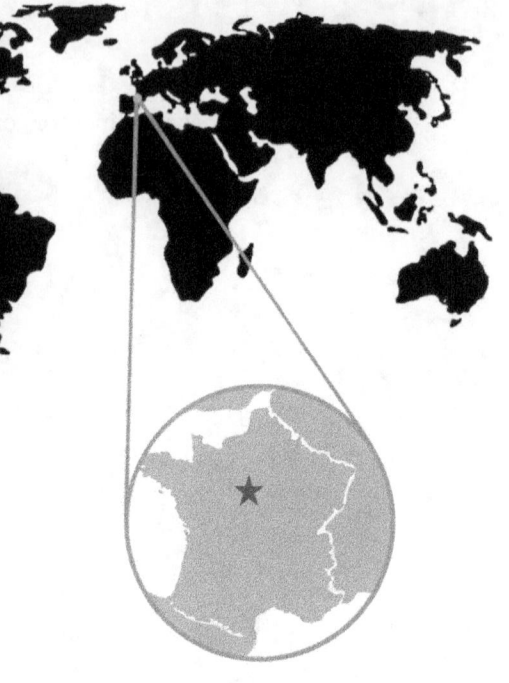

- The Louvre has to employ a small army, over 2,000 employees, to maintain the museum and its artwork.

- The Louvre has served several purposes over the centuries, including a fortress and a palace. Believe it or not, it was left abandoned and fell into disrepair when the French royal court moved to the Palace of Versailles.

- The Louvre actually displays less than 10% of its entire collection! Around 35,000 works are on display at a time. The remaining pieces of the total collection of over 380,000 are kept in storage.

- The Louvre has started to open satellite museums under "The Louvre" name, which will share and display the vast collection of works owned by the museum. Locations include Lens, France and Abu Dhabi, United Arab Emirates (planned completion 2015).

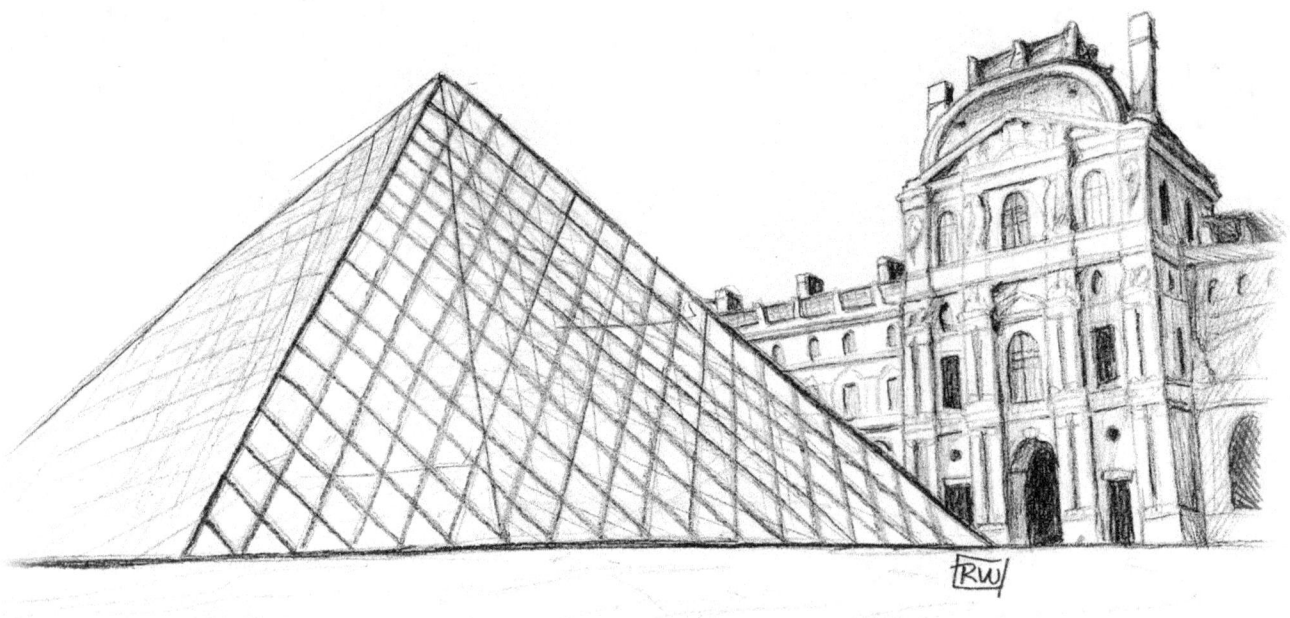

TIP:

Remember areas left light or white should be touched by the light source. Those that are darker should indicate shadow.

Machu Picchu

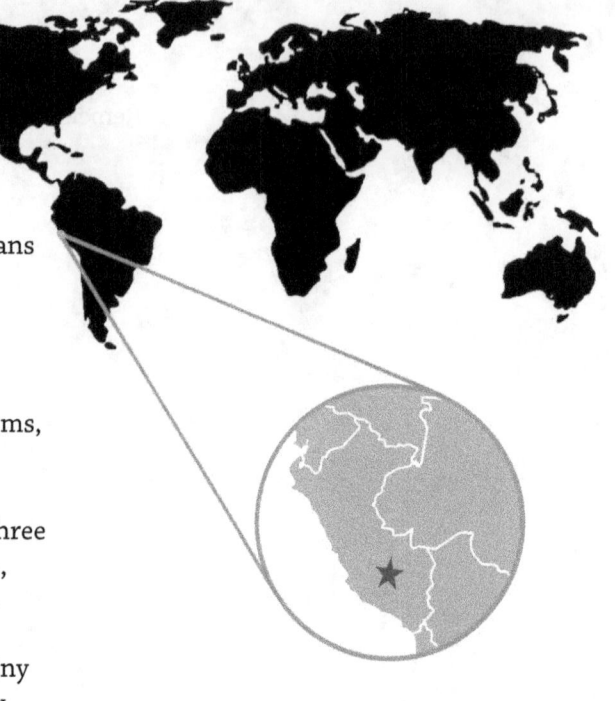

- In the native language of Quechua, "Machu Picchu" means "Old Peak" or "Old Mountain".

- The city has stood resistance to the effects of regular earthquakes. This is due to the amazing engineering techniques such as mortar-free walls, inward tilting rooms, and rounded corners used during construction.

- The most popular method to get to Machu Picchu is a three day trek up to 7,970 feet (2,430 meters) on stone paths, and the use of a local guide, or a "porter", is mandatory.

- You will often find porters sleeping with a mirror or shiny object to ward off spirits they fear will whisk them away.

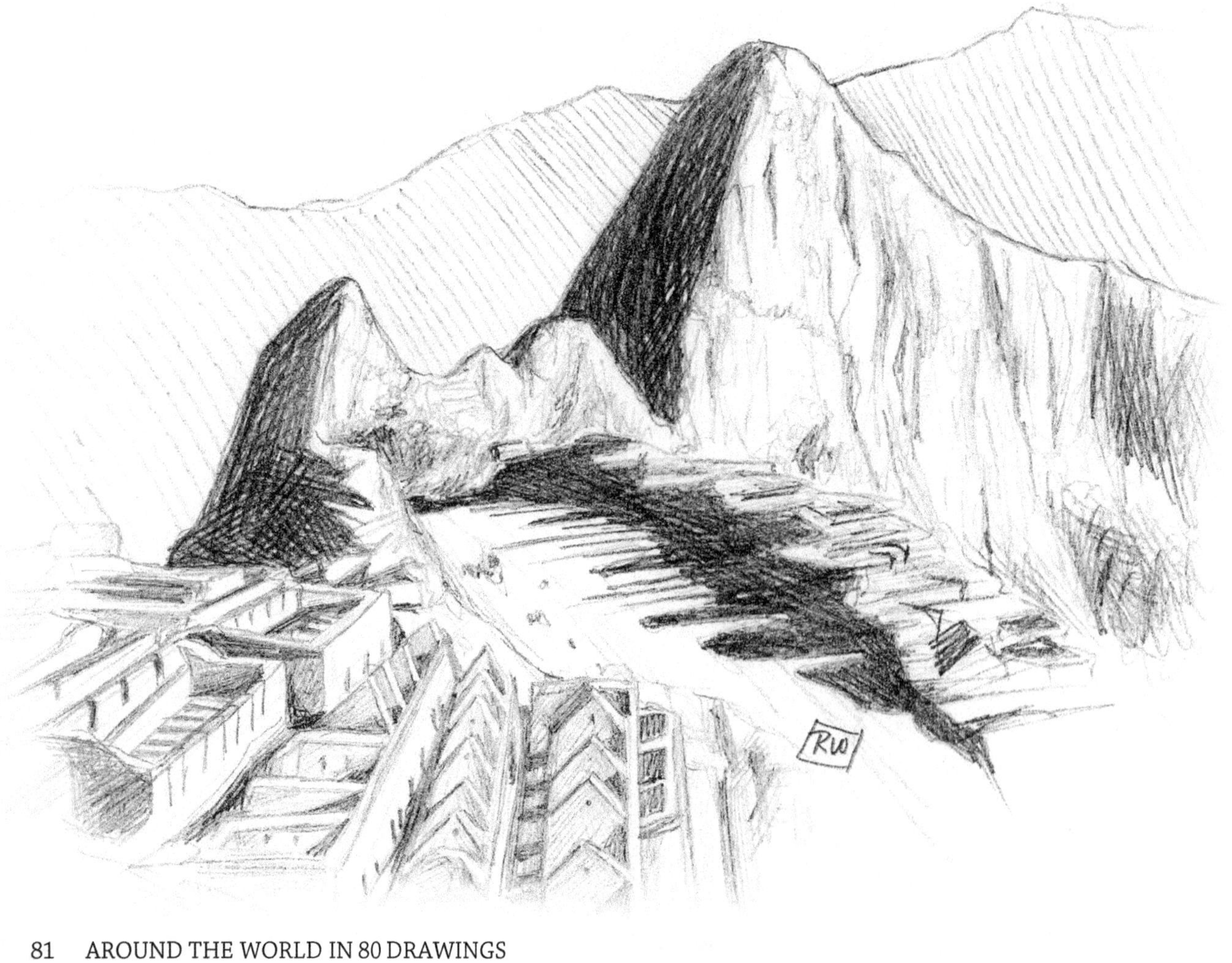

TIP:
Landscapes can be detailed differently to create different textures.

Milan Cathedral

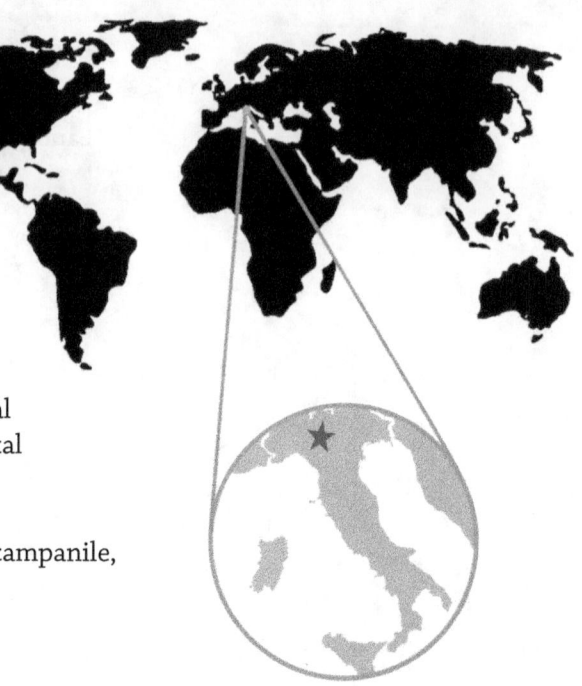

- The Milan cathedral has around 135 spires, each mounted with a statue depicting biblical characters, as well as people of importance to the history of Milan.

- It's been said that there are more statues on the Cathedral of Milan than on any other structure in the world; the total sits at around 3,159 statues.

- Although many European churches have a bell tower, or campanile, the Duomo of Milan does not.

- The Duomo is literally at the center of Milan. The city streets radiate from the cathedral, circling it.

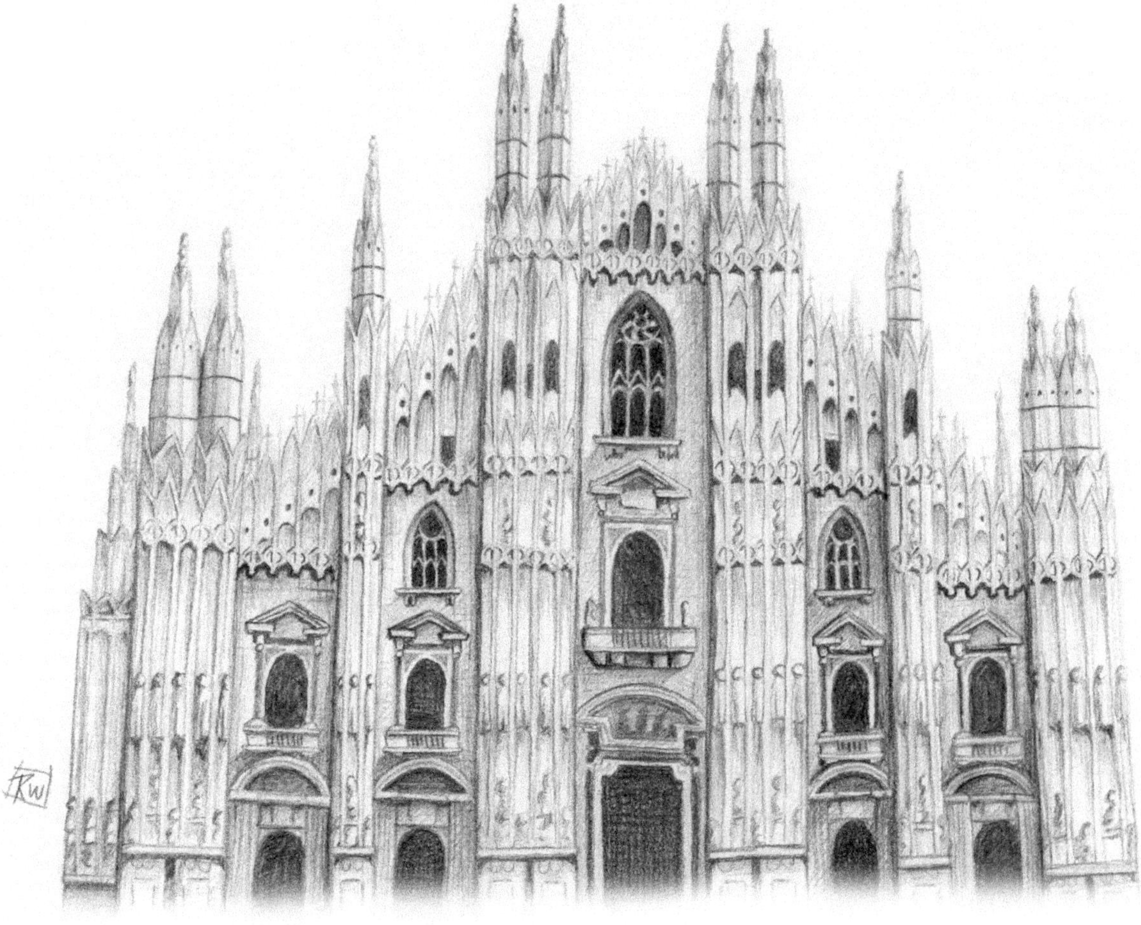

Simple shading gives the smoothest looking quality to the sketch's surface.
Don't be afraid to experiment as there are many different pencil grades.

Moai Statues

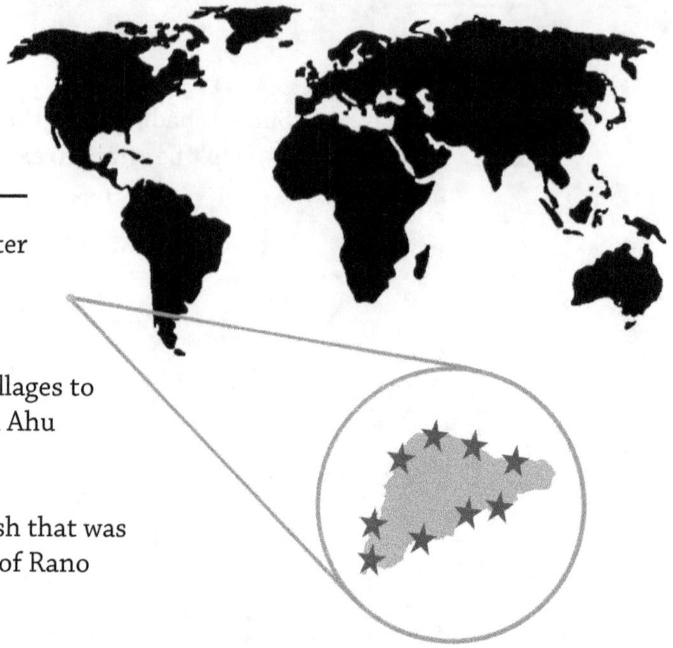

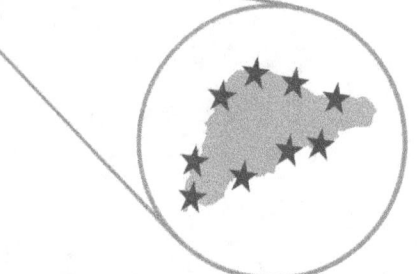

- Although more commonly referred to as "the Easter Island Heads", the Moai are actually fully bodied statues that have been buried up to their necks.

- It is believed the Moai statues face towards the villages to watch over the people, except for seven statues in Ahu Akivi which face the sea to help those navigating.

- The statues are carved out of solidified volcanic ash that was excavated from a quarry near the extinct volcano of Rano Raraku.

- Easter Island is one of the world's most famous archeological sites, yet the least visited.

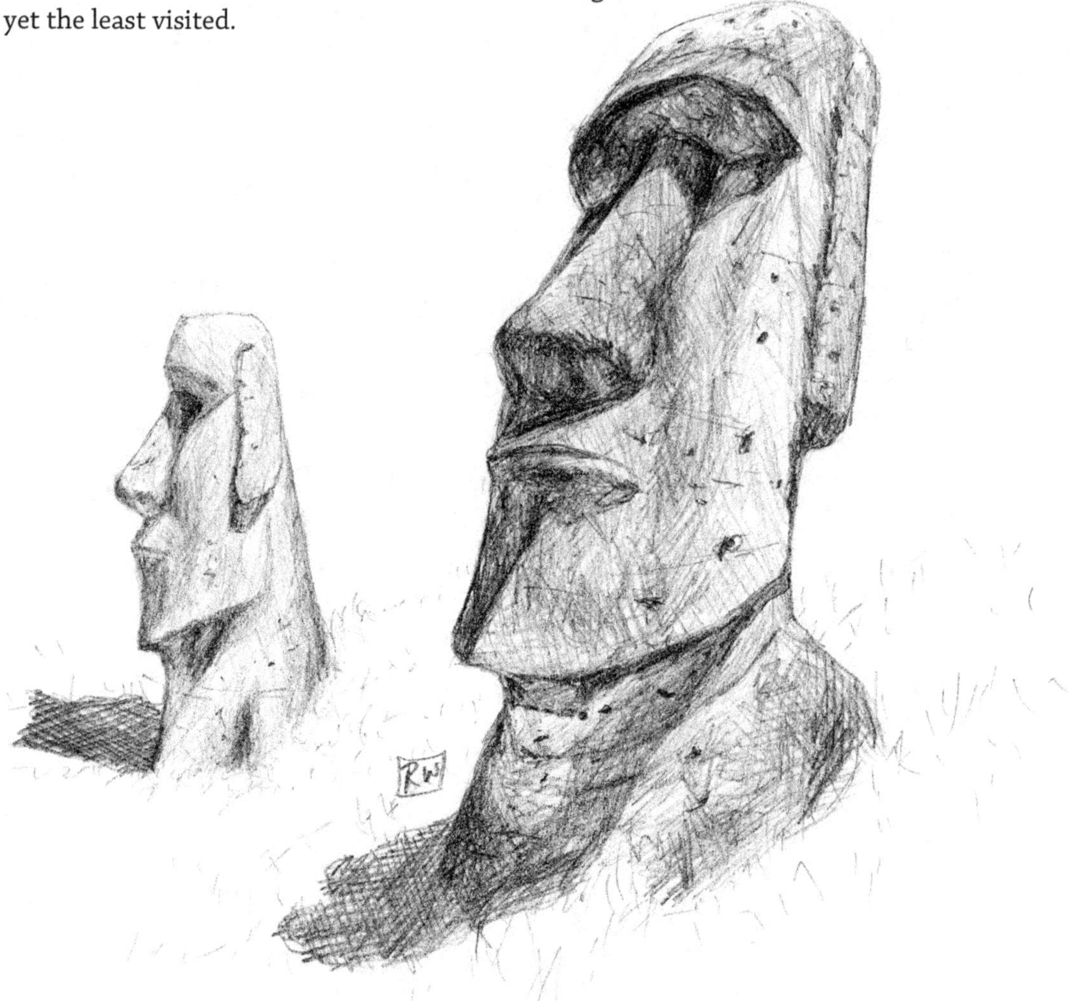

TIP:

Don't get overwhelmed, look for basic shapes in the object you are sketching.
Start with the basics, then elaborate.

Mont Saint-Michel

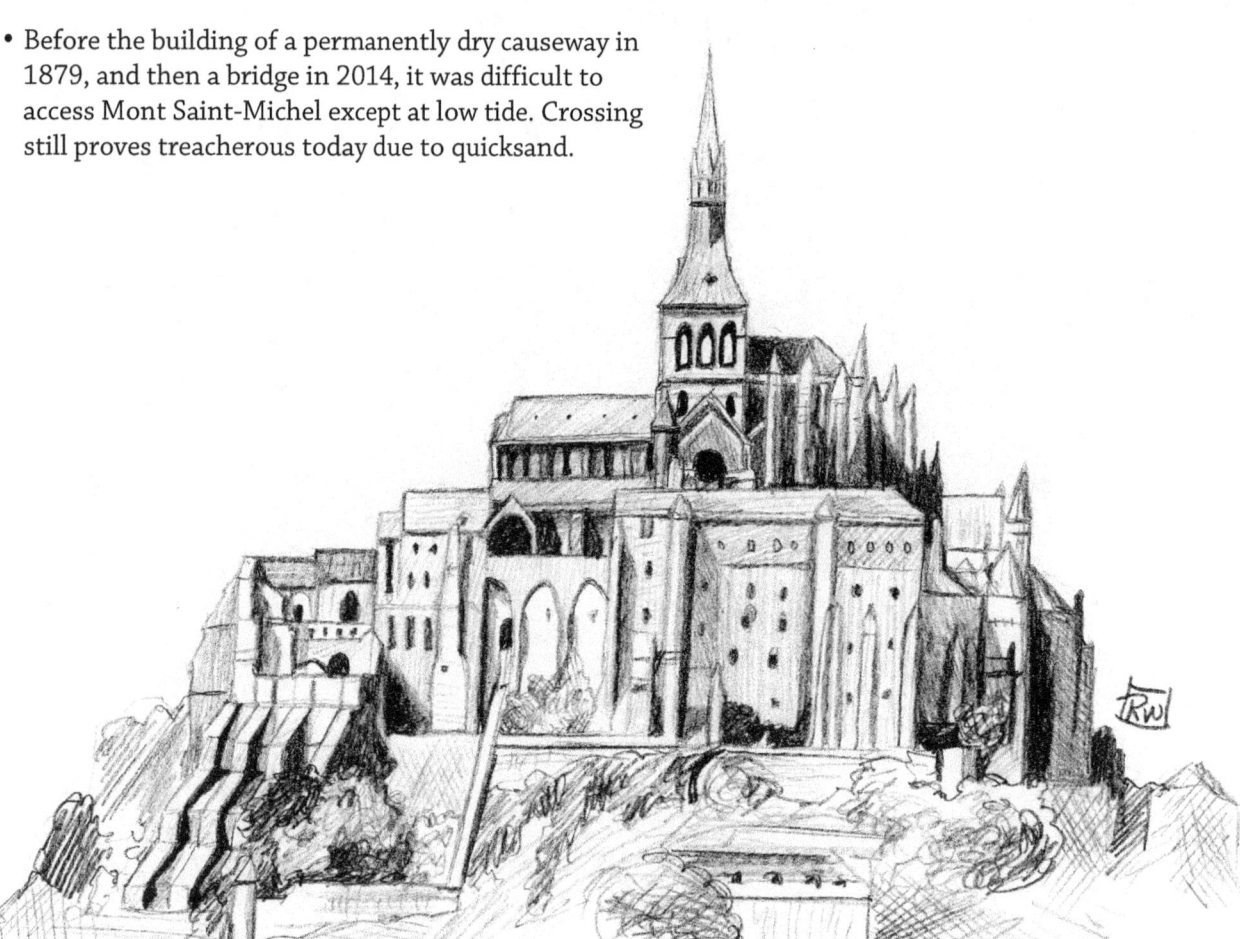

- In 708 AD, according to legend, the Archangel Michael appeared to the local bishop of Avranches and advised him to "build here and build high."

- Since the 8th century, the island has been structured as a medieval society, with the abbey and monastery signifying God at the peak. The great hall and stores are just below, followed by the housing and fishermen's villages towards the lower part of the island.

- As the island of Mont Saint-Michel has the natural defenses of high tide and dense fog, the monastery repeatedly served as an effective prison over the centuries.

- Before the building of a permanently dry causeway in 1879, and then a bridge in 2014, it was difficult to access Mont Saint-Michel except at low tide. Crossing still proves treacherous today due to quicksand.

If the structure has a lot of detail, take your time and sketch an outline first.

Monument Valley

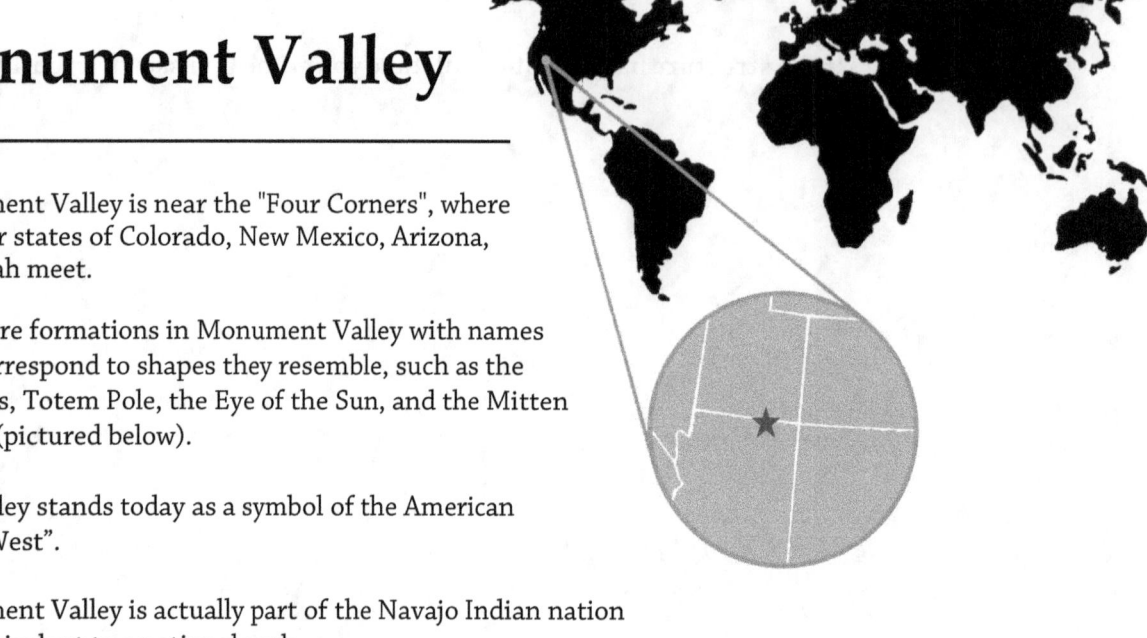

- Monument Valley is near the "Four Corners", where the four states of Colorado, New Mexico, Arizona, and Utah meet.

- There are formations in Monument Valley with names that correspond to shapes they resemble, such as the 3 sisters, Totem Pole, the Eye of the Sun, and the Mitten Buttes (pictured below).

- The valley stands today as a symbol of the American "Wild West".

- Monument Valley is actually part of the Navajo Indian nation and equivalent to a national park.

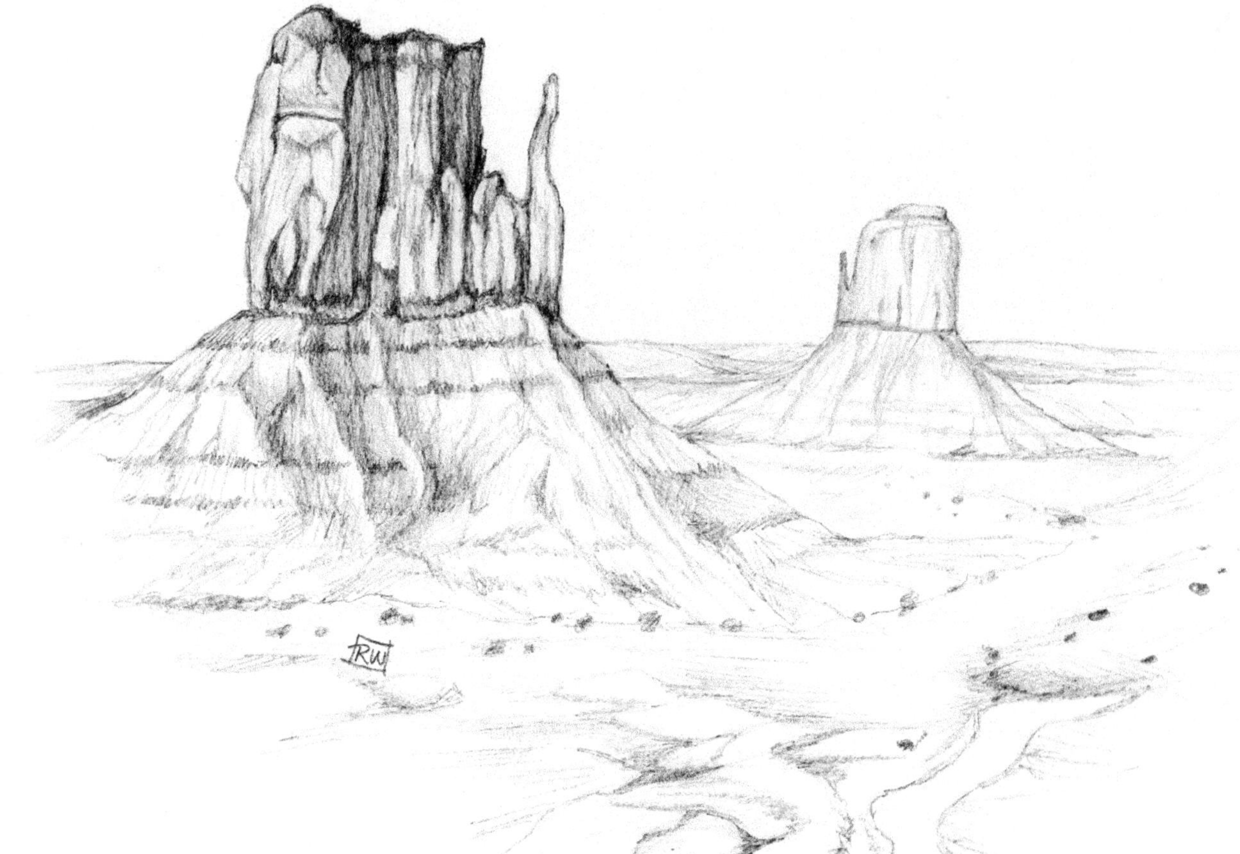

Remember to have fun with it and embellish with creative marks every now and then.
A pencil in your hand is freedom for you imagination.

Moulin Rouge

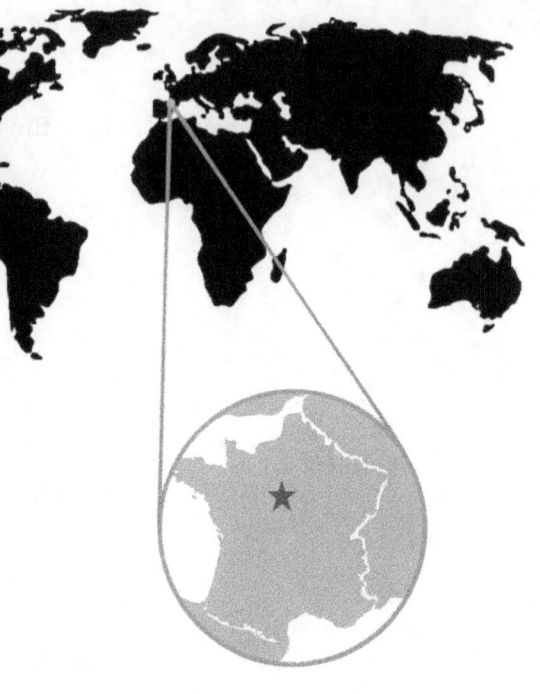

- The Moulin Rouge is known as the birthplace for the modern Can-can dance.

- Moulin Rouge carries the façade of a large red windmill that is a tribute to the history of the Montmartre district; once a village with many windmills.

- Moulin Rouge can be found in the district of Montmartre, which was considered a place where all walks of life could come and enjoy Paris: artists, middle class, businessmen, elegant women, foreigners, etc.

- Although opened in 1889, Moulin Rouge is still used today offering musical and dance entertainment for visitors from all over the world.

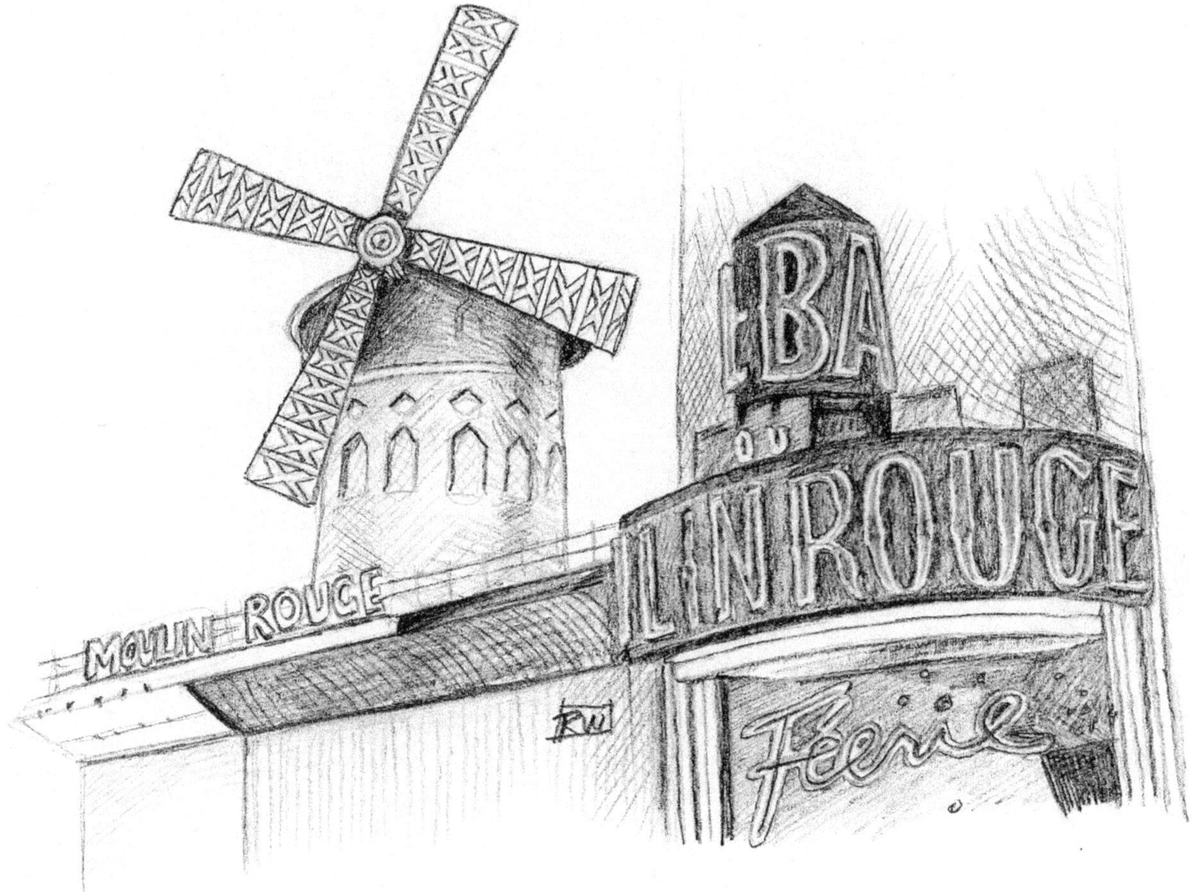

TIP:
Good drawings have a full range of value.
Use various shades of light and dark for your sketch to seem realistic.

Mount Kilimanjaro

- It is the world's highest free-standing mountain, at nearly 20,000 feet (5,895 meters) above sea level.

- Kilimanjaro is also known as the "Roof of Africa".

- Uhuru Peak is the highest summit and is home to a wooden box where climbers can leave their deepest thoughts.

- Kilimanjaro is home to six different ecological systems: cultivated land, rainforest, heath, moorland, alpine desert, and the arctic summit.

- Coffee is grown on the lower slopes of the mountain and used as a major export.

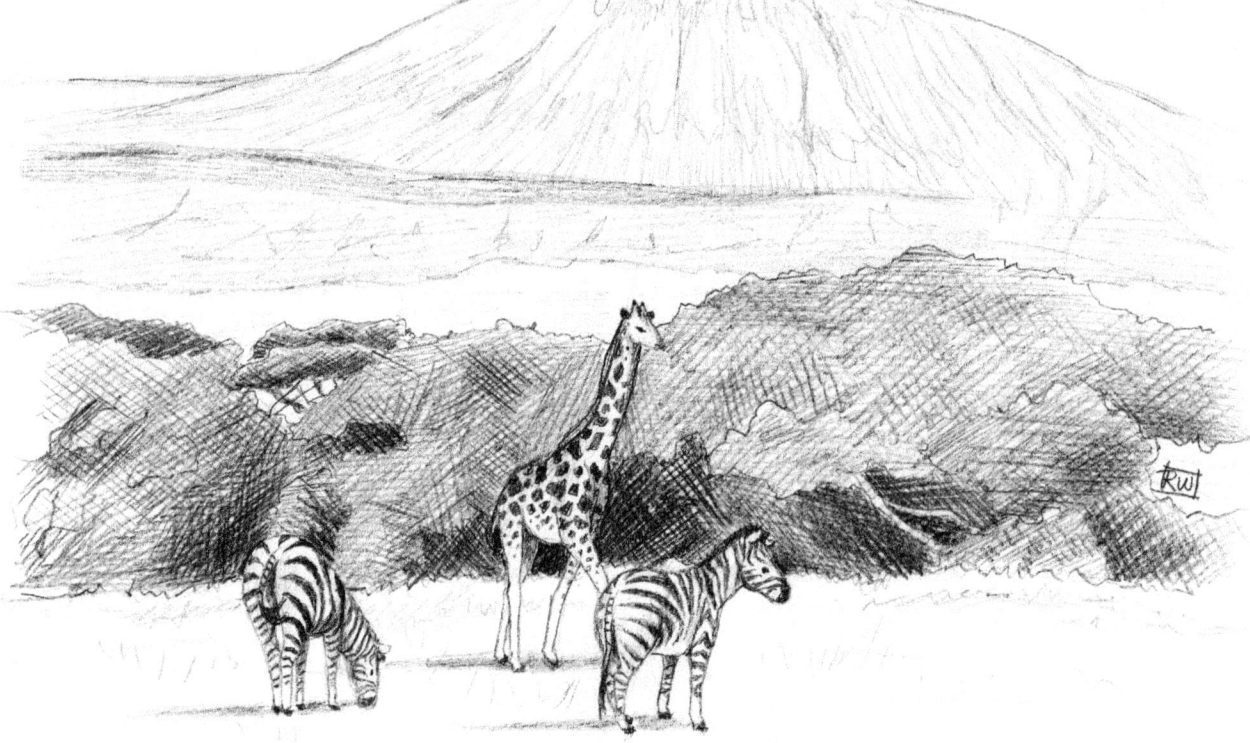

TIP:

Don't try to draw every blade of grass or leaf, it will leave your sketch looking unnatural. Instead, use light, feathery strokes to sketch the suggestion of grass or leaves.

Naqsh-e Jahan Square

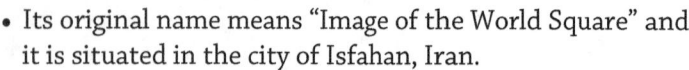

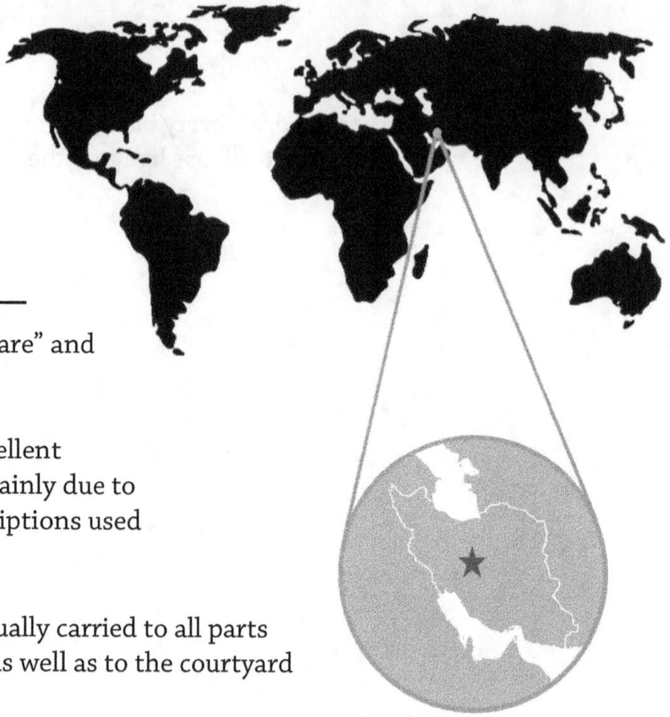

- Its original name means "Image of the World Square" and it is situated in the city of Isfahan, Iran.

- The Shah Mosque was built in 1611 and is an excellent example of Islamic architecture with its beauty mainly due to the seven-color mosaic tiles and calligraphic inscriptions used throughout.

- The acoustics inside are amazing and sound is equally carried to all parts of the dome chamber and cloisters on each side, as well as to the courtyard and the lateral porches

- Across the square sits the Sheikh Lotfallah Mosque, which displays a unique feature on its dome. The center of the dome is adorned with a peacock, and a hole in the ceiling allows sunrays to enter and portray the tail feathers of the peacock.

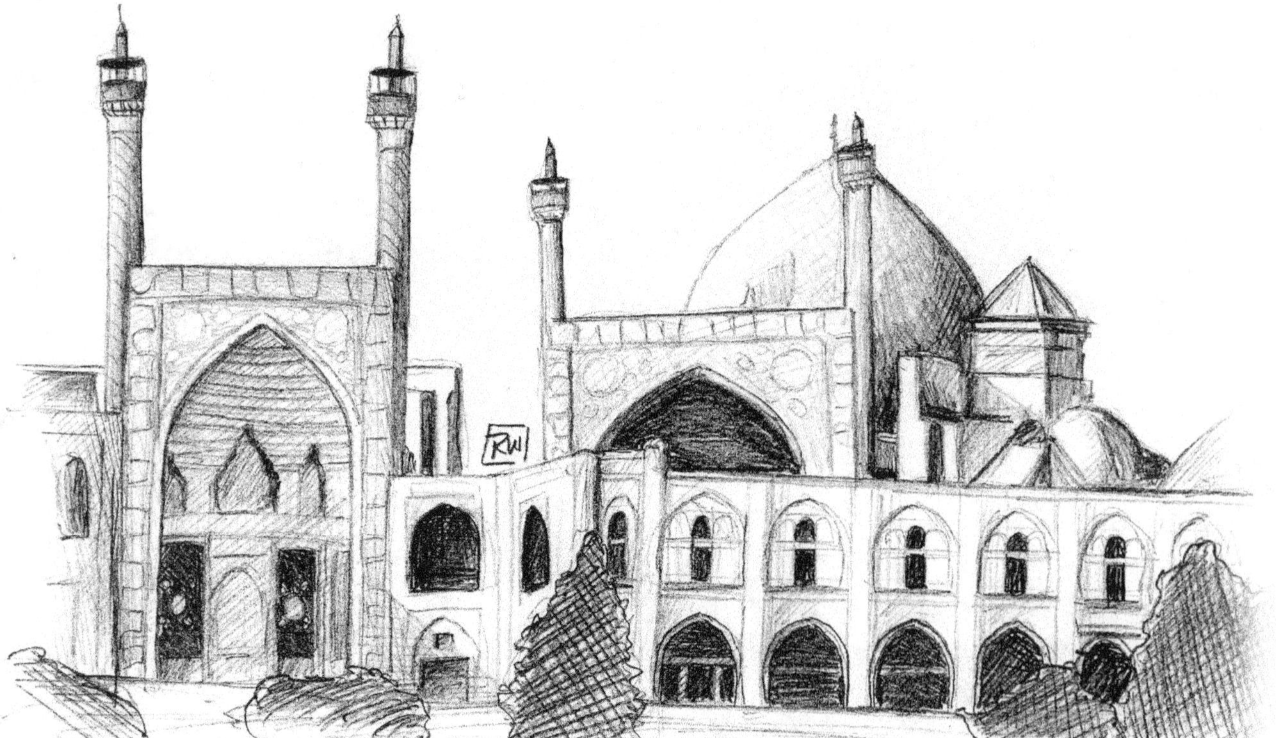

Niagara Falls

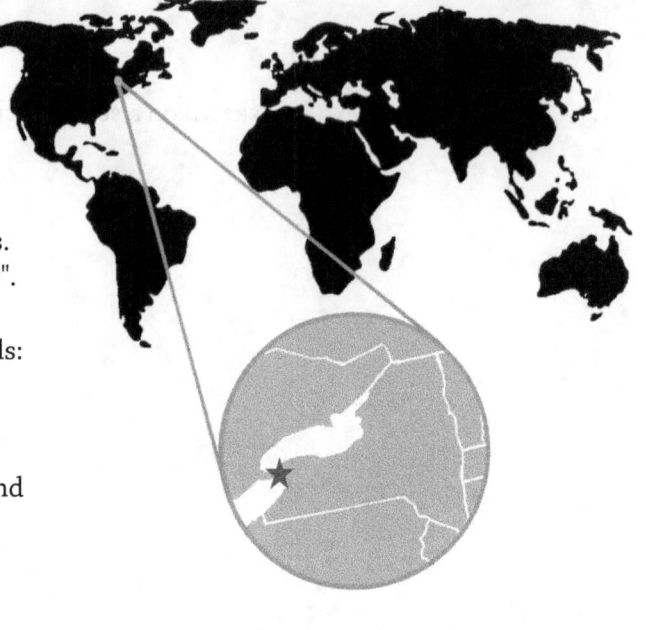

- The word "Niagara" comes from the Iroquois Indians. The Indian term is "Onguiaahra" meaning "the strait".

- Niagara Falls is compiled of three groups of waterfalls: the American Falls, the Bridal Veil Falls and the Horseshoe Falls.

- 3,160 tons of water flowing at a rate of 32 feet/second flows over Niagara Falls every second.

- On March 29th, 1848 due to an ice jam in the upper Niagara River, the falls did not actually freeze solid, but the flow of water stopped enough for people to walk along the mouth of the falls.

- The Niagara Falls State Park is the oldest state park in the United States, being established in 1885.

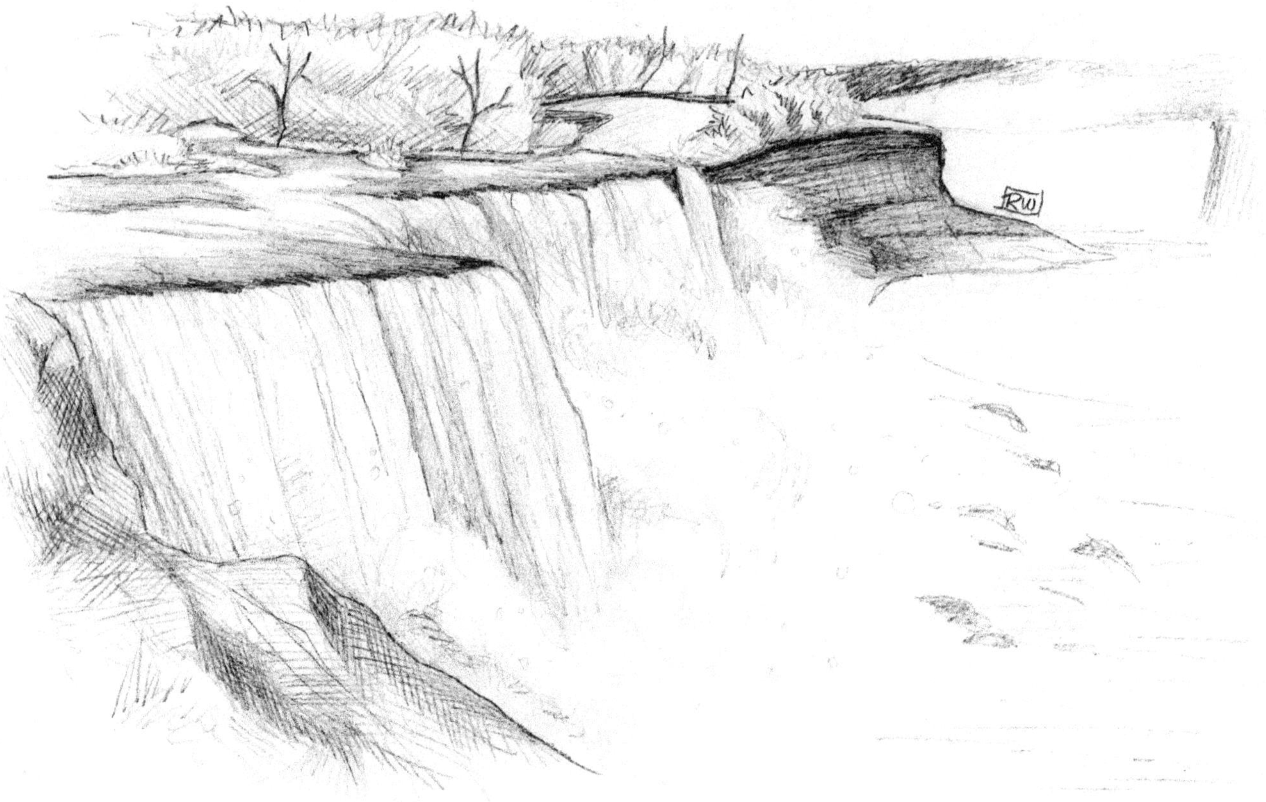

TIP:
Water in motion is difficult to capture.
By adding mist and clouds at the base, it gives the illustion the water is moving quickly.

Neuschwanstein Castle

- Though it hosts over 6,000 visitors a day, Neuschwanstein Castle was never finished; only about 15 rooms and halls in the palace were actually completed.

- It took almost 5 years and 15 carpenters just to carve the elaborate woodwork that can now be seen in the King's chamber.

- The Nazi Party used the palace as a location to store stolen works of art from France during World War II.

- Neuschwanstein Castle was the inspiration for the Sleeping Beauty Castle at Disneyland Park in California.

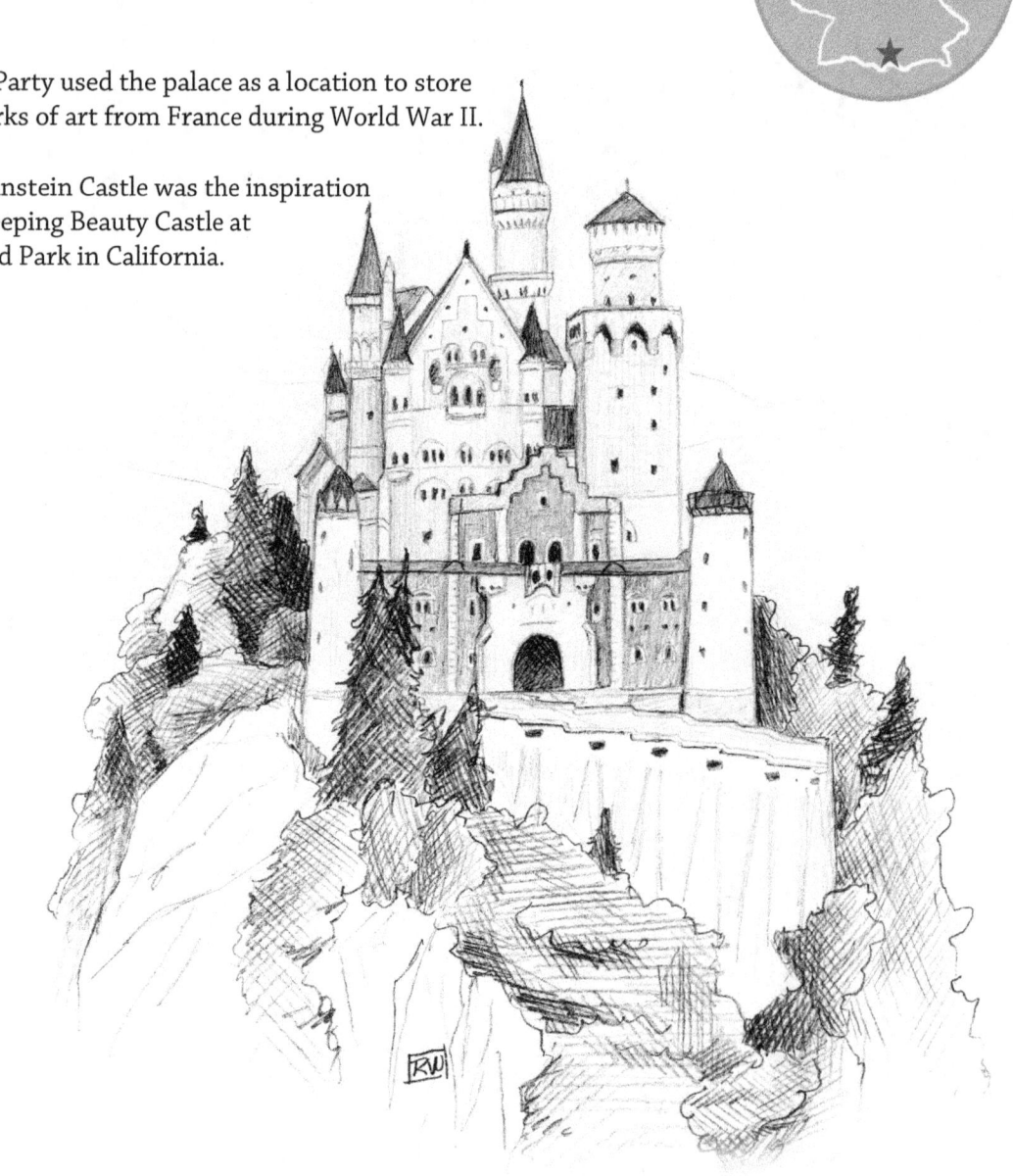

TIP:
Don't be afraid to leave the sketch with no background.
Sometimes it's best to just focus on the subject.

Notre-Dame Cathedral

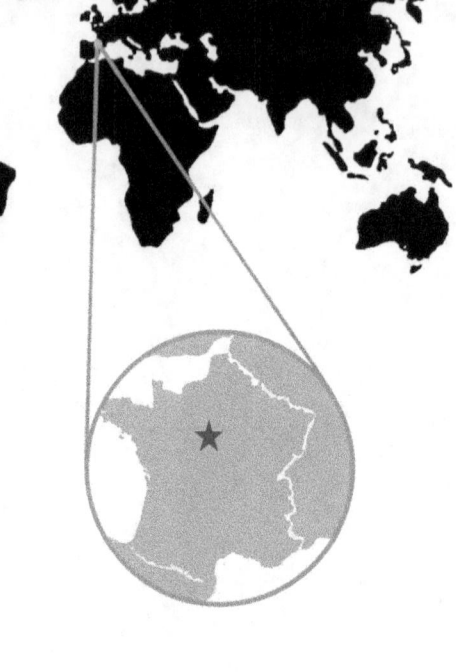

- Although you won't find a hunchback in the bell towers of Notre-Dame, you will find the largest bell called "Emmanuel", which weighs over 13 tons! This bell is always rung first; five seconds before the rest.

- Notre-Dame Cathedral was once painted in vivid colors, which have worn off over the years.

- Although many believe the gargoyles of Notre-Dame to be strictly decoration, they also serve as rain spouts diverting rain water off of the roof to help avoid damage.

- During the French Revolution, the cathedral was used for food storage.

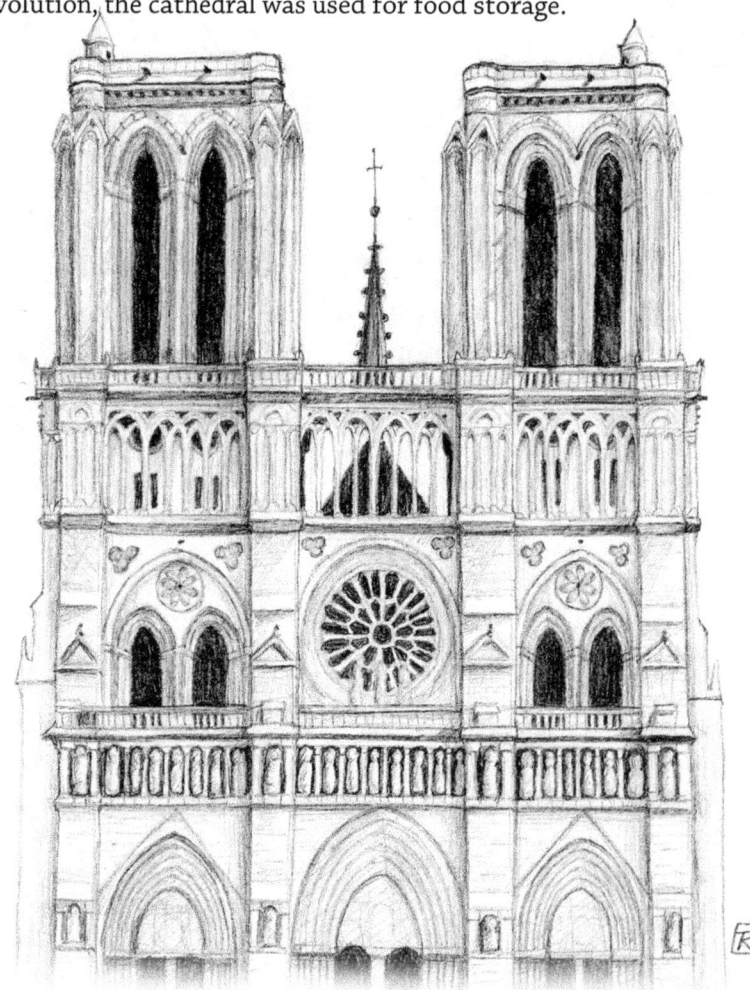

Palace of Versailles

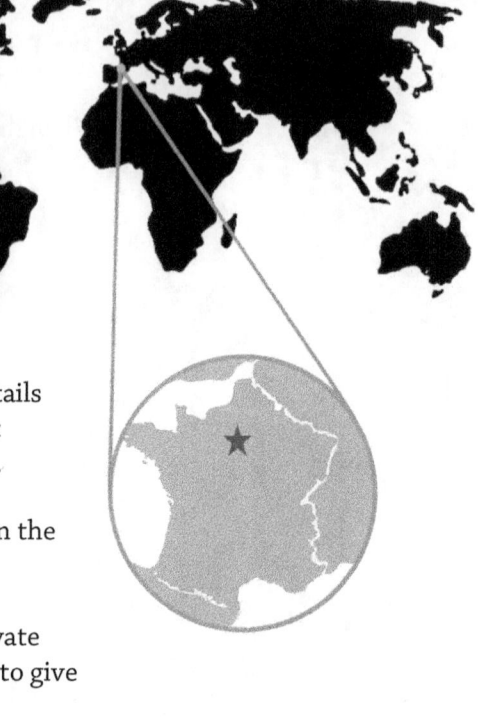

- The Palace of Versailles was upgraded from a simple hunting lodge, to a lavish palace with over 700 rooms, 50 fountains, and almost 2,000 acres of gardens, over its lifetime!

- Lighting was used sparingly in the palace to protect the ornate details on the walls and ceilings. Mirrors were often used to amplify what little light was present, thus the famed Hall of Mirrors came to be.

- The Treaty of Versailles, to end World War I, was actually signed in the Hall of Mirrors inside the palace.

- The Queen's room, or bedchamber, is one of the largest of the private apartments. This was due to the fact that the queen was expected to give birth in public, and the rooms needed to accommodate onlookers.

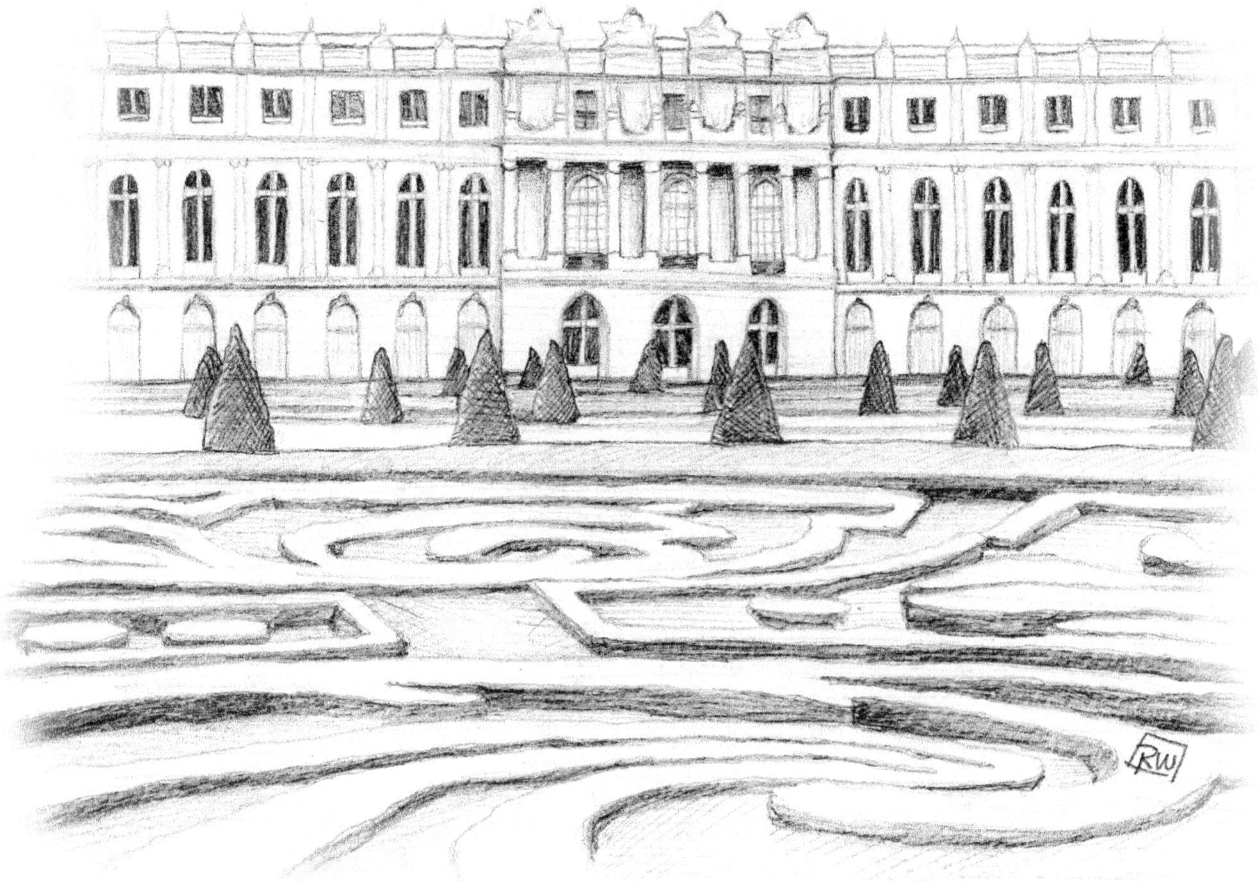

TIP:
Perspective should always be taken into consideration.
Try to find an angle or perspective that is unique and interesting.

Parliament Hill

- It is said there is a secret stairwell in the West Block. When Alexander Mackenzie was the Canadian prime minister, from 1873 to 1878, he had an office which included a secret escape route to avoid lobbyists.

- There is a fountain that surrounds the Centennial Flame at the entrance of Parliament Hill. Every year the coins thrown in the fountain are collected and used to help fund research for various disabilities

- Until 1955, cats were used to keep the rodents under control in the Parliament buildings. In 1970, a cat sanctuary was opened where stray cats could go to live and eat.

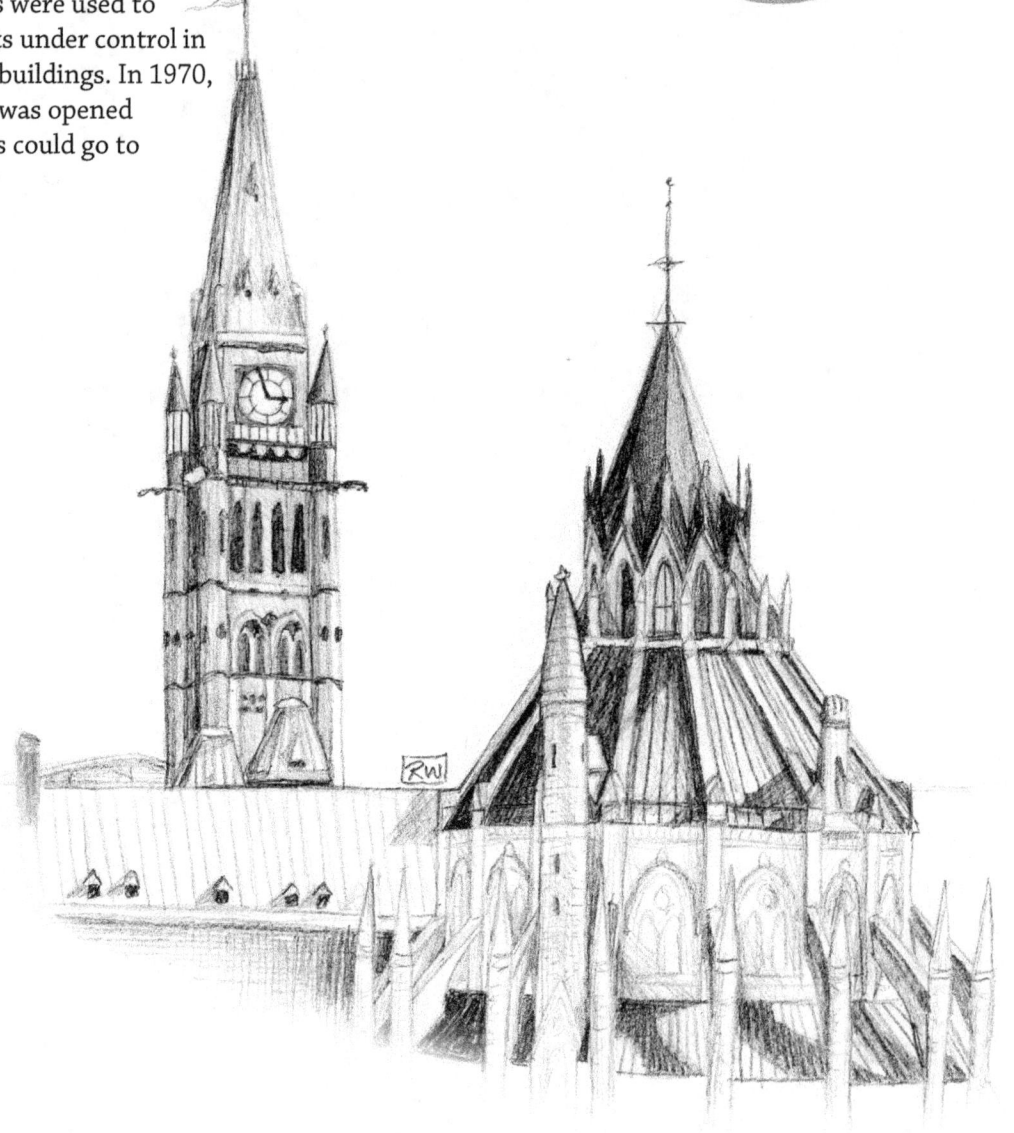

TIP:
Avoid resting your hand on your drawing; it will smudge the graphite.
Instead, use a piece of scrap paper under your hand if you need to rest.

Parthenon

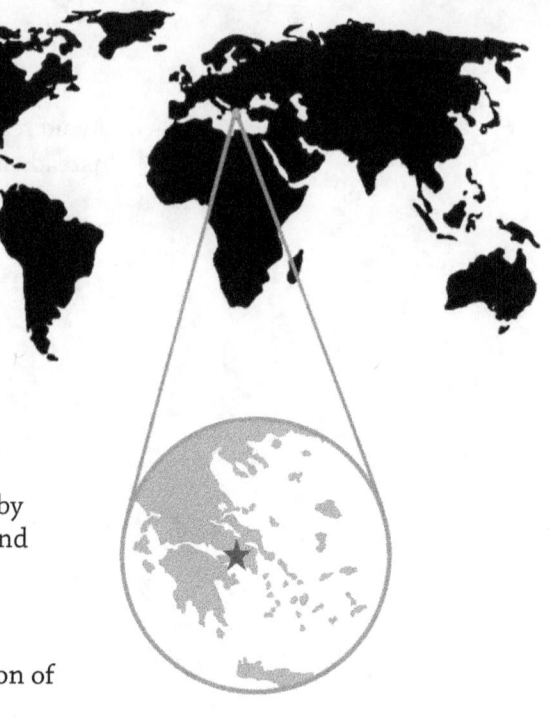

- The Parthenon is part of the Athenian Acropolis that sits upon a hill above Athens; "Acro", meaning "high" and "polis", meaning "city".

- The Parthenon is a temple that was built to honor the Greek goddess of wisdom, Athena.

- Inside the Parthenon was a giant statue of Athena designed by the sculptor Phidias and is said to have been made of ivory and gold; it was dedicated around 438 BC.

- The Parthenon has served multiple purposes as a church, a mosque and a munitions depot during the Turkish Occupation of Greece.

- A full-scale replica of the original Parthenon was built in 1897 and is located in Nashville, Tennessee.

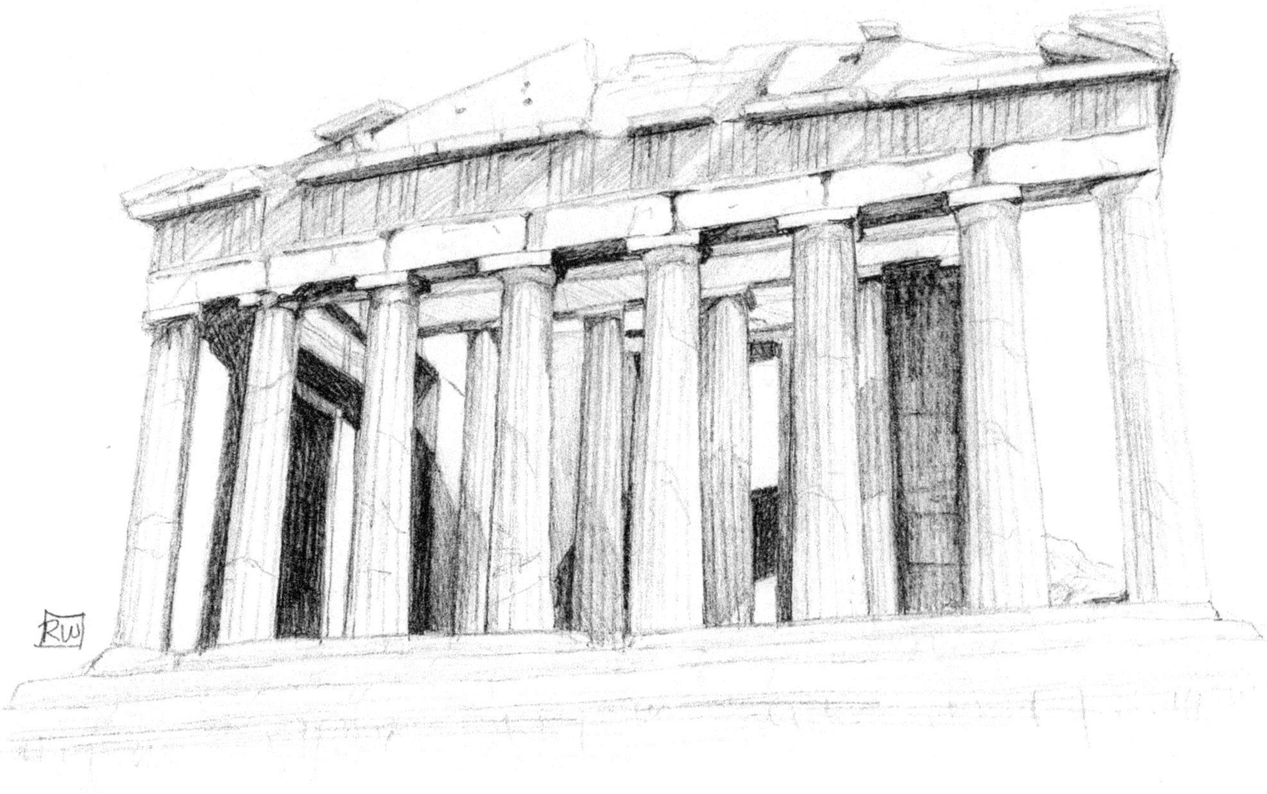

TIP:
Draw your lines thicker in some places and thinner in others.
Variance in line quality adds interst and variety to your sketch.

Penguins in Antarctica

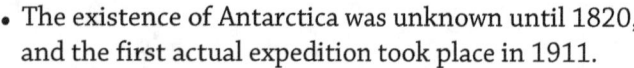

- The existence of Antarctica was unknown until 1820, and the first actual expedition took place in 1911.

- There are no countries in Antarctica; the continent is governed by an international treaty.

- Although the temperatures have been measured as cold as -128.6°F (-89.2°C), Antarctica is technically considered a desert due to its lack of significant precipitation.

- It is the coldest, windiest, highest, and driest continent on the planet.

- The Emperor penguin is the only species of penguin that breed during the Antarctic winter. The male penguins actually incubate the single egg, while the females trek some 30-75 miles (50–120 km) to fish and build up a food storage to feed the chick, once hatched.

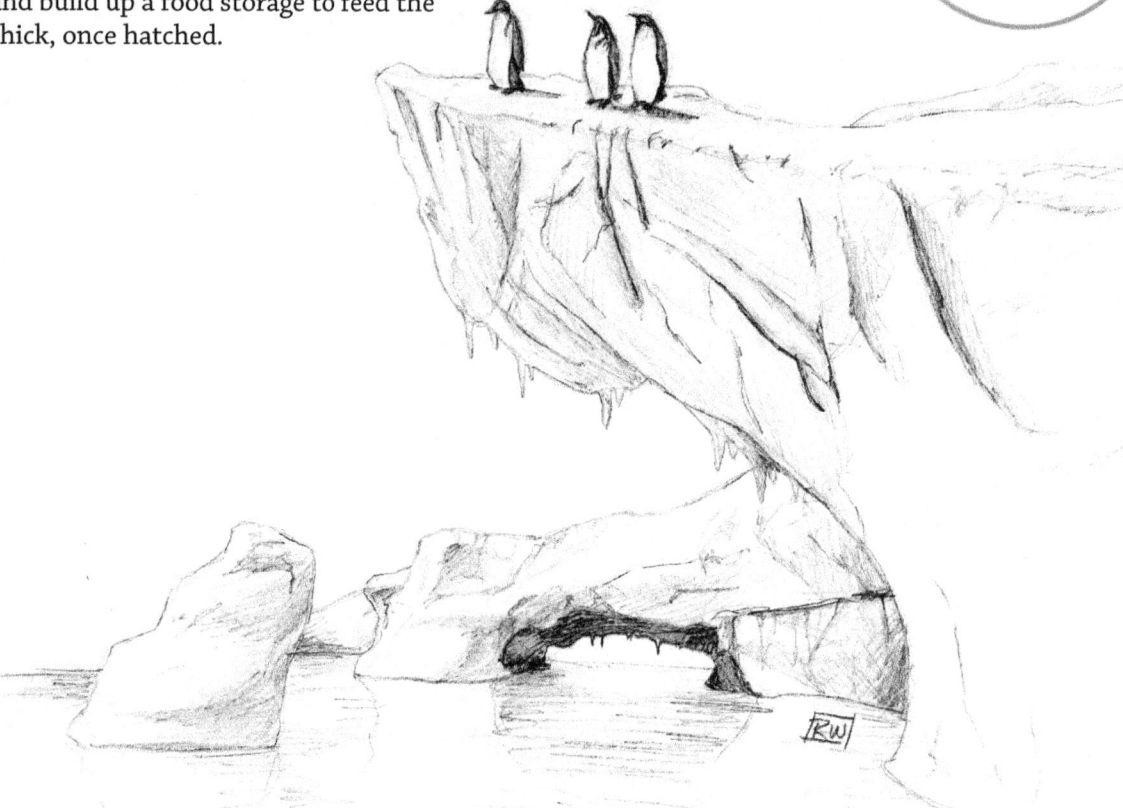

TIP:
Give a sense of scale whenever possible.
Put in an animal or person to show just how big or small a structure or object is.

Petra

- Petra is also known as "the Rose City" because of the color of the stone from which it's carved.

- Although the city is said to have been built around 312 BC, it was not known to the Western world until 1812, when it was rediscovered by Swiss explorer, Johann Ludwig Burckhardt.

- The main access to Petra is through a narrow gorge known as "The Siq". It is approximately ¾ of a mile long (1.2 km), 300-597 feet (91-182 meters) high, and in some places is no wider than a claustrophobic 9 feet (3 meters)!

- If you stick around after dark, you can marvel in the city's glow as the lights of over 1,000 candles dance on the red stone of the structure.

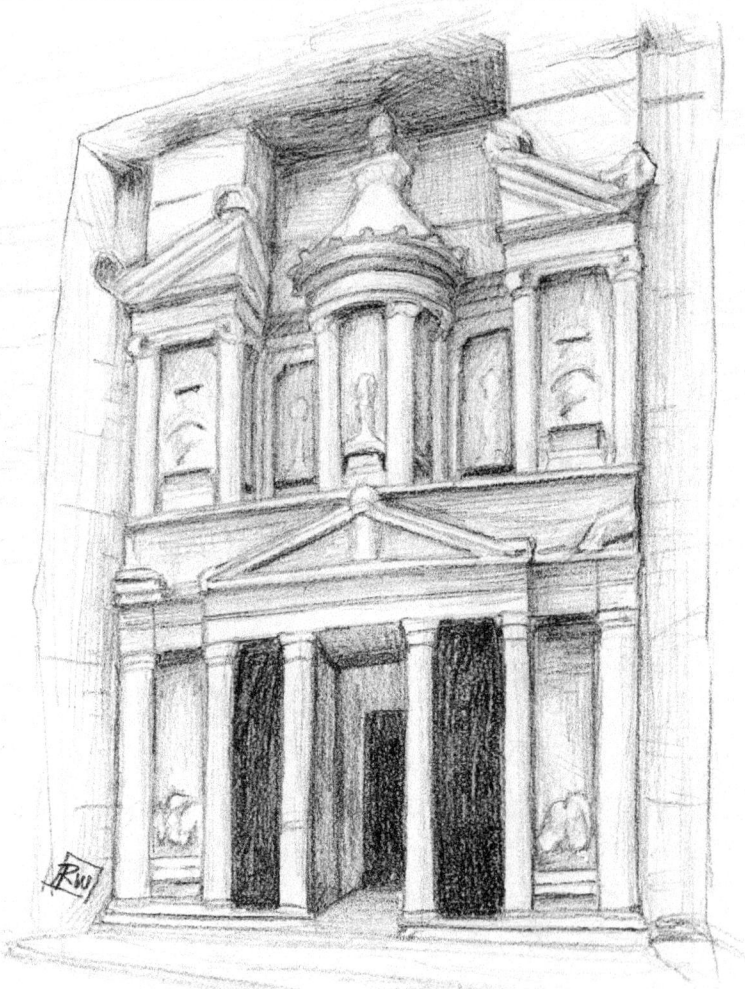

Petronas Twin Towers

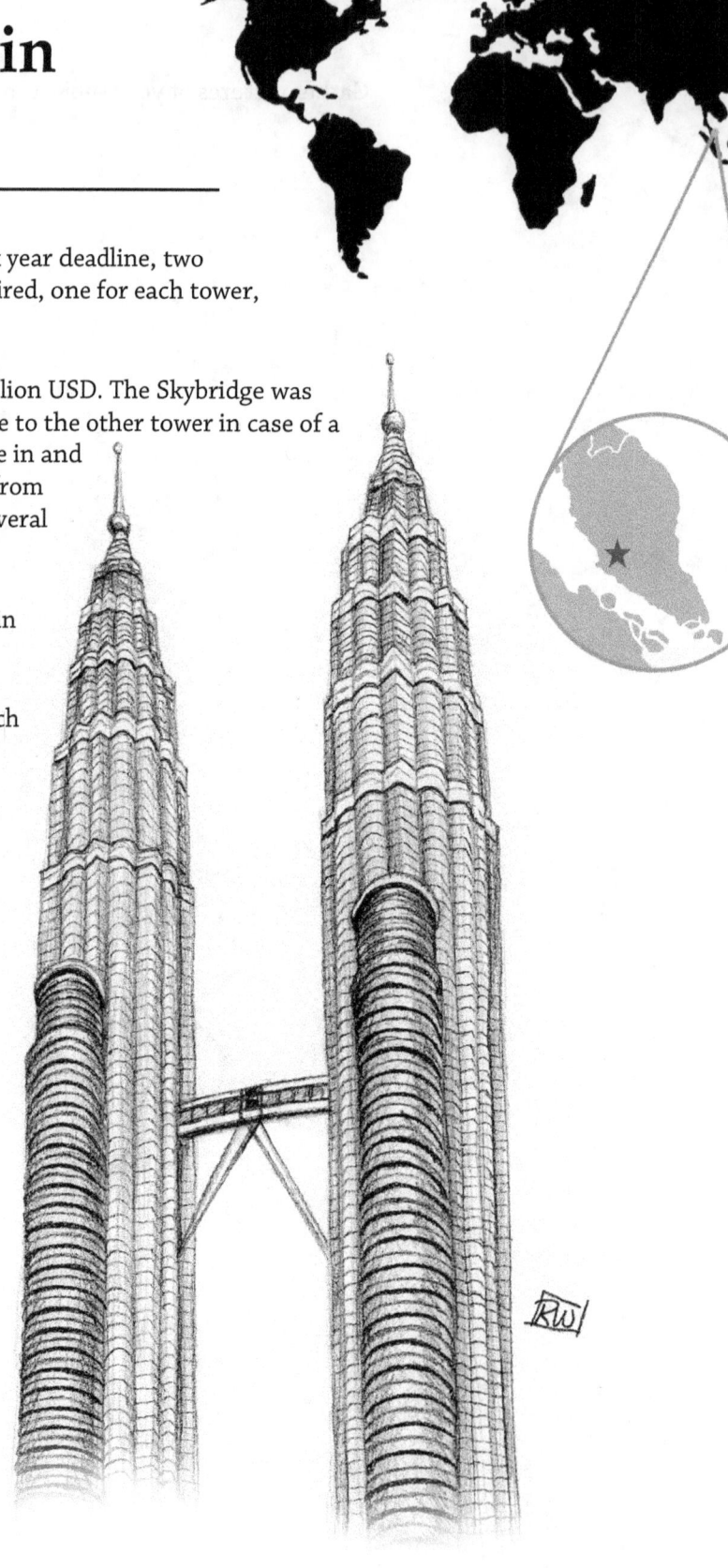

- In order to meet a very tight six year deadline, two construction companies were hired, one for each tower, racing each other to the top.

- The building costs were $1.8 billion USD. The Skybridge was built to allow occupants to move to the other tower in case of a fire. It was also designed to slide in and out of the towers to prevent it from breaking, as the towers sway several feet during high winds.

- They were the tallest buildings in the world from 1998 to 2004.

- In order to stay on schedule, each floor had to be constructed in four days.

Find a style that is your own and stick with it throughout the duration of your sketch.

Ponte Vecchio

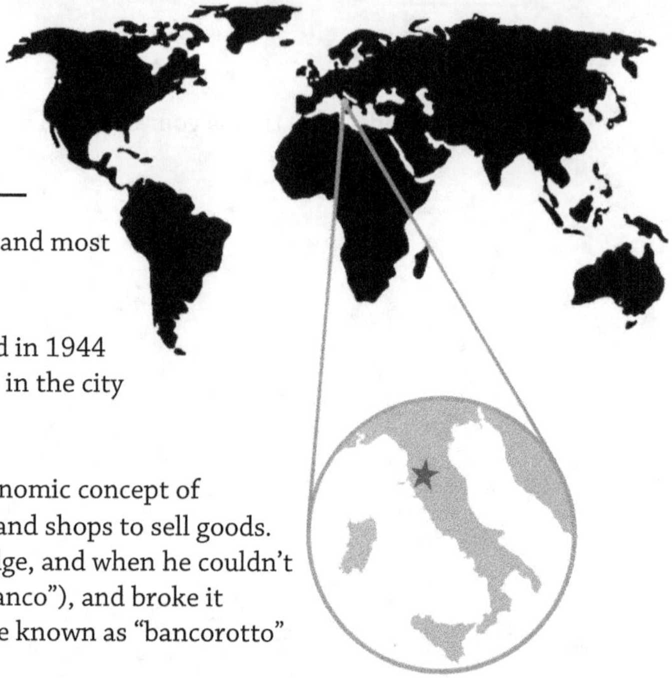

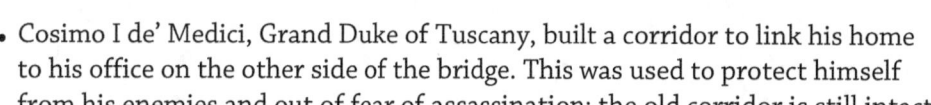

- Ponte Vecchio was built in 1345 and is the oldest and most iconic bridge in Florence.

- It was spared by the Germans when they retreated in 1944 at the end of World War II, while all other bridges in the city were destroyed.

- Ponte Vecchio could be the birth place for the economic concept of "bankruptcy". The bridge was used by merchants and shops to sell goods. It is said a debt-ridden man had a stall on the bridge, and when he couldn't pay his debts, law officials took his shop table ("banco"), and broke it ("rotto") to prohibit business. The practice became known as "bancorotto" or "broken table".

- Cosimo I de' Medici, Grand Duke of Tuscany, built a corridor to link his home to his office on the other side of the bridge. This was used to protect himself from his enemies and out of fear of assassination; the old corridor is still intact.

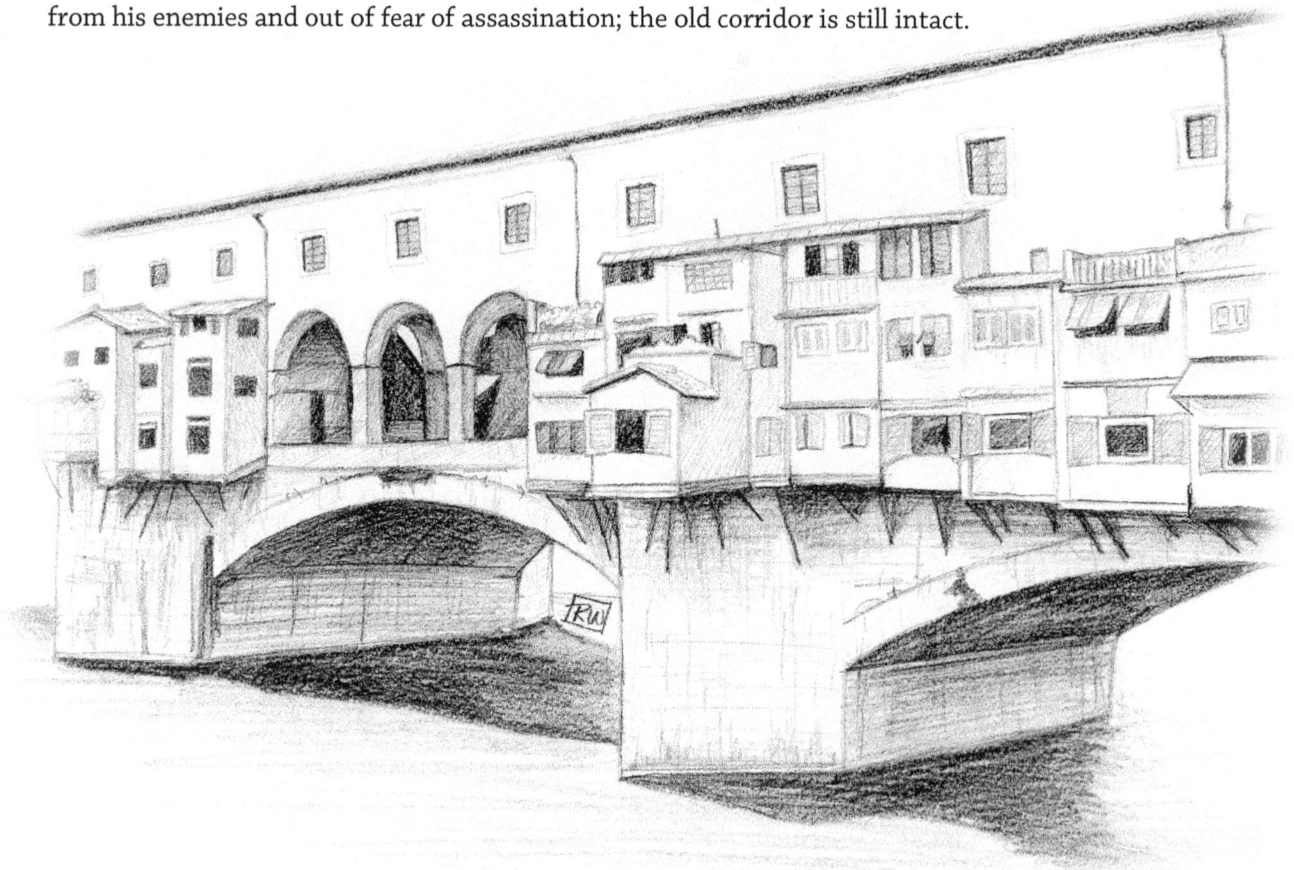

Techniques like hatching ▨ cross-hatching ▨ , and scrumbling ▨ add texture to your sketch.

Roman Forum

- The Roman Forum was the central area of the city around which Rome developed.

- For centuries this was the site of the most important public buildings where various activities took place: commerce, business, elections, public speeches, trials, religious gatherings and more.

- Foro was the name that the Romans gave to the central square.

- Over the lifetime of the Forum, wealthy men regularly added statues, buildings and artwork to the grounds commemorating the city's great men.

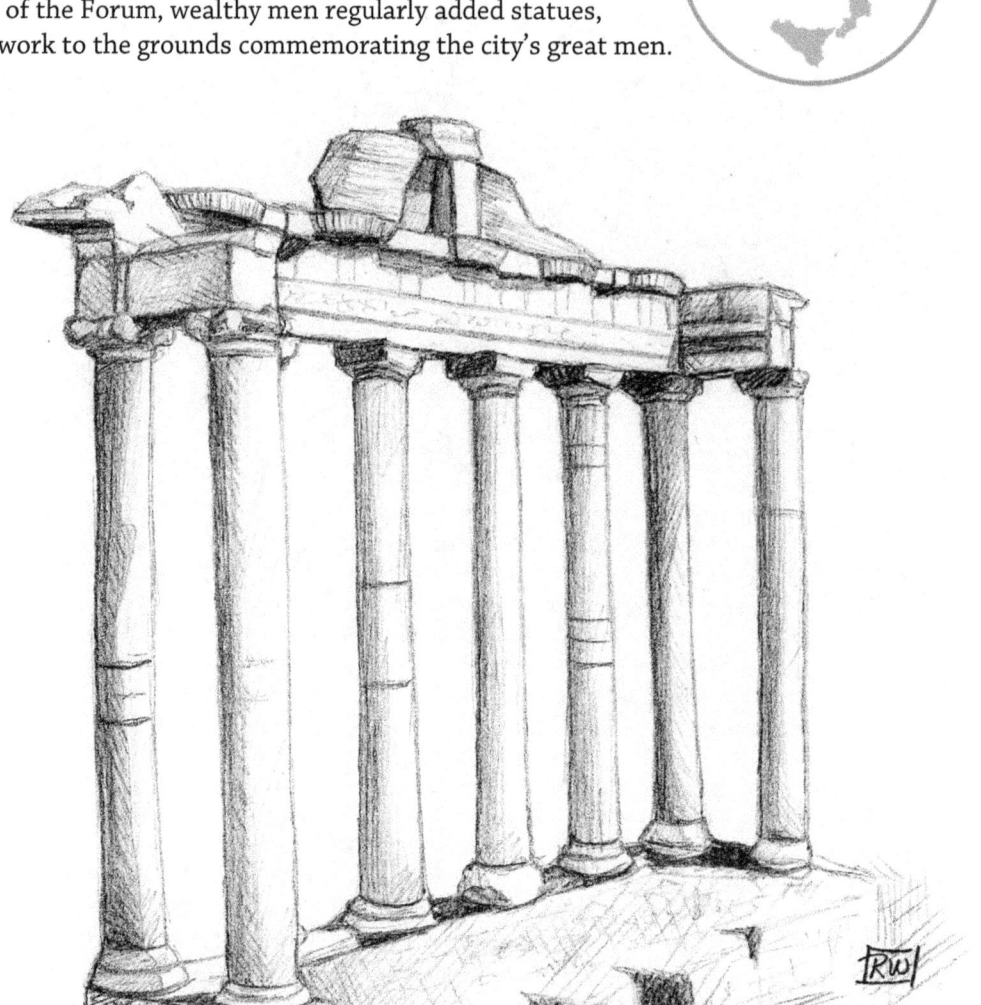

TIP:
Sometimes less is more; don't feel the need to capture every element of a scenic sketch.

Running of the Bulls

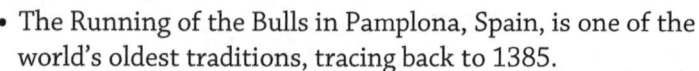

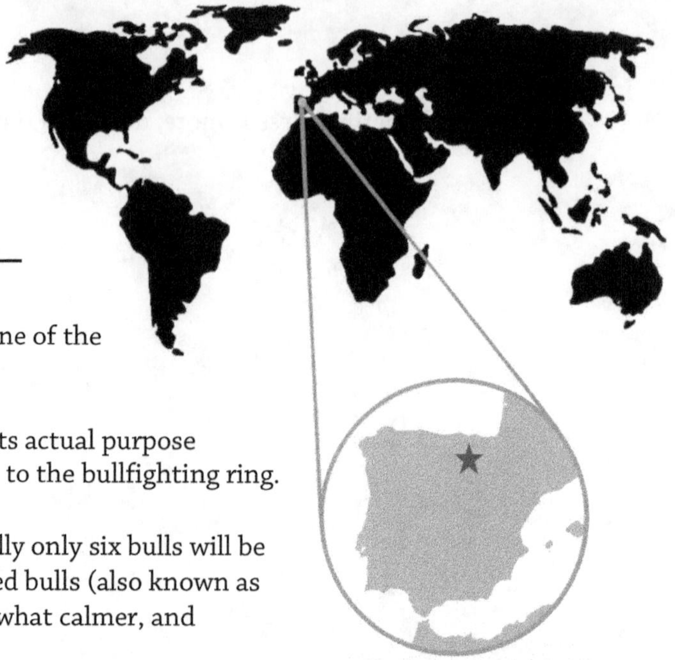

- The Running of the Bulls in Pamplona, Spain, is one of the world's oldest traditions, tracing back to 1385.

- The Running of the Bulls is not only a risky feat, its actual purpose was to transport the bulls from Pamplona's corral to the bullfighting ring.

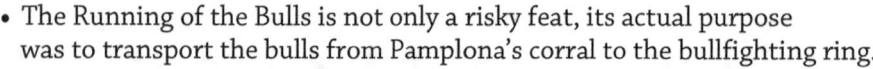

- While it is named "the Running of the Bulls" usually only six bulls will be released into the streets, along with a few castrated bulls (also known as steers). The steers are said to keep the bulls somewhat calmer, and therefore, make the run less dangerous.

- The run itself only takes about three minutes on average every day over the course of a week-long festival in July.

- Those who choose to run with the bulls and wear the traditional white pants and white shirt with a red scarf are called "Mozos." Despite common belief, bulls are color blind, so the color red does not actually anger them.

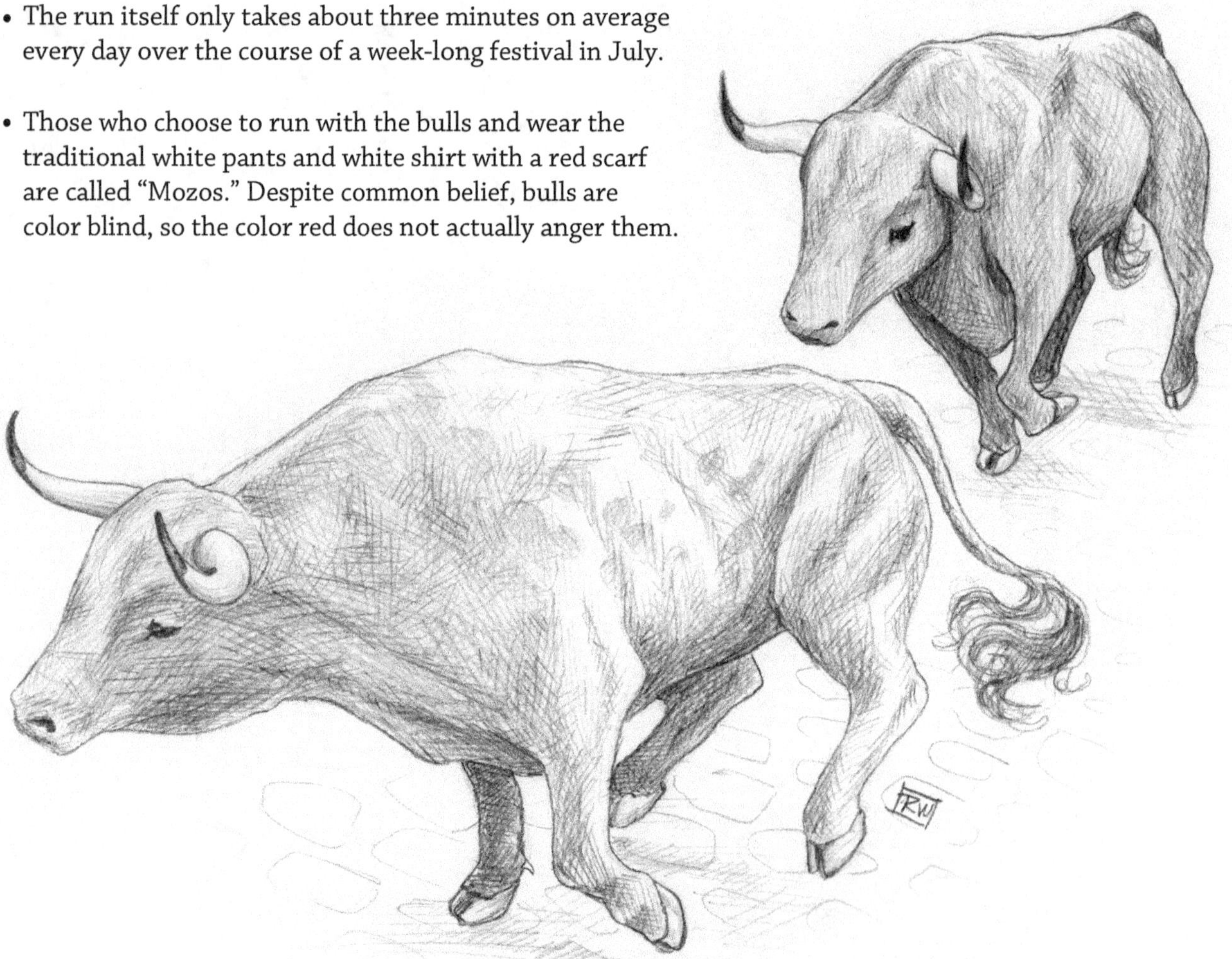

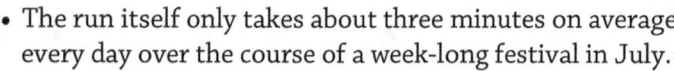

TIP:

Sketching animals can be tricky.
To keep them realistic, be sure you keep in mind the natural curves of the animal's body.

Sacré-Coeur

- The Sacré-Couer basilica is dedicated to the Sacred Heart of Jesus and is located in the city of Paris, France.

- Due to its location on the hill of Montmartre, the basilica towers over the city; its highest point is even higher than the top of the Eiffel Tower, affording spectacular views of Paris.

- The hill is a very significant place in history, and has always been a sacred site since pre-Christian times. The present basilica was built in 1876.

- The Sacré-Coeur is constructed of stone from Château-Landon. This type of stone constantly seeps out calcite, allowing the monument to maintain its white color, despite the weather and pollution of the city.

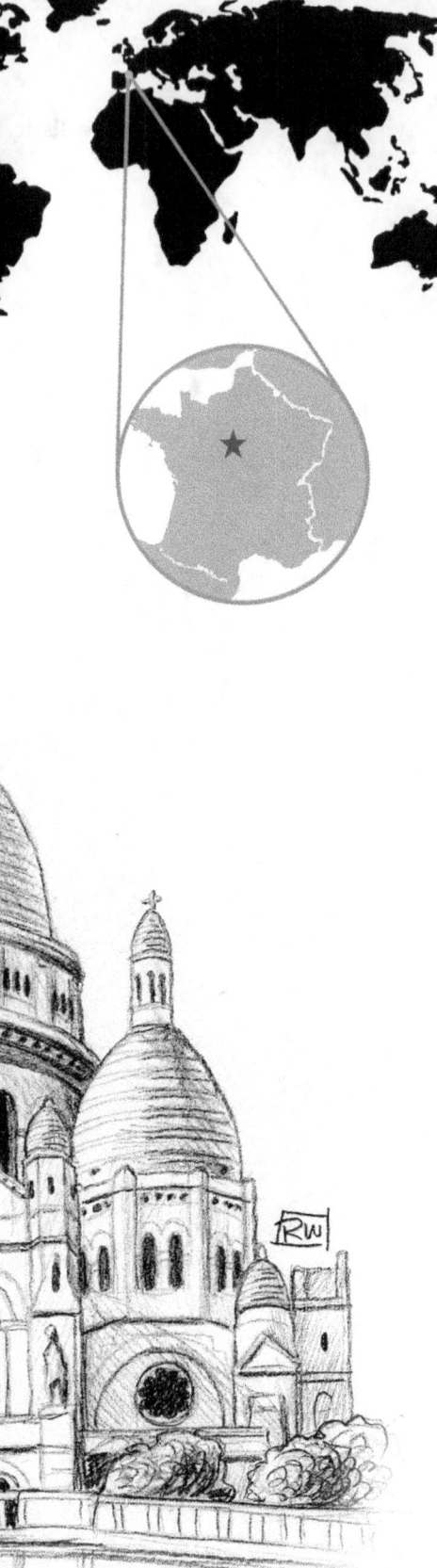

TIP:
A sharp pencil makes drawing small details easier.

La Sagrada Familia

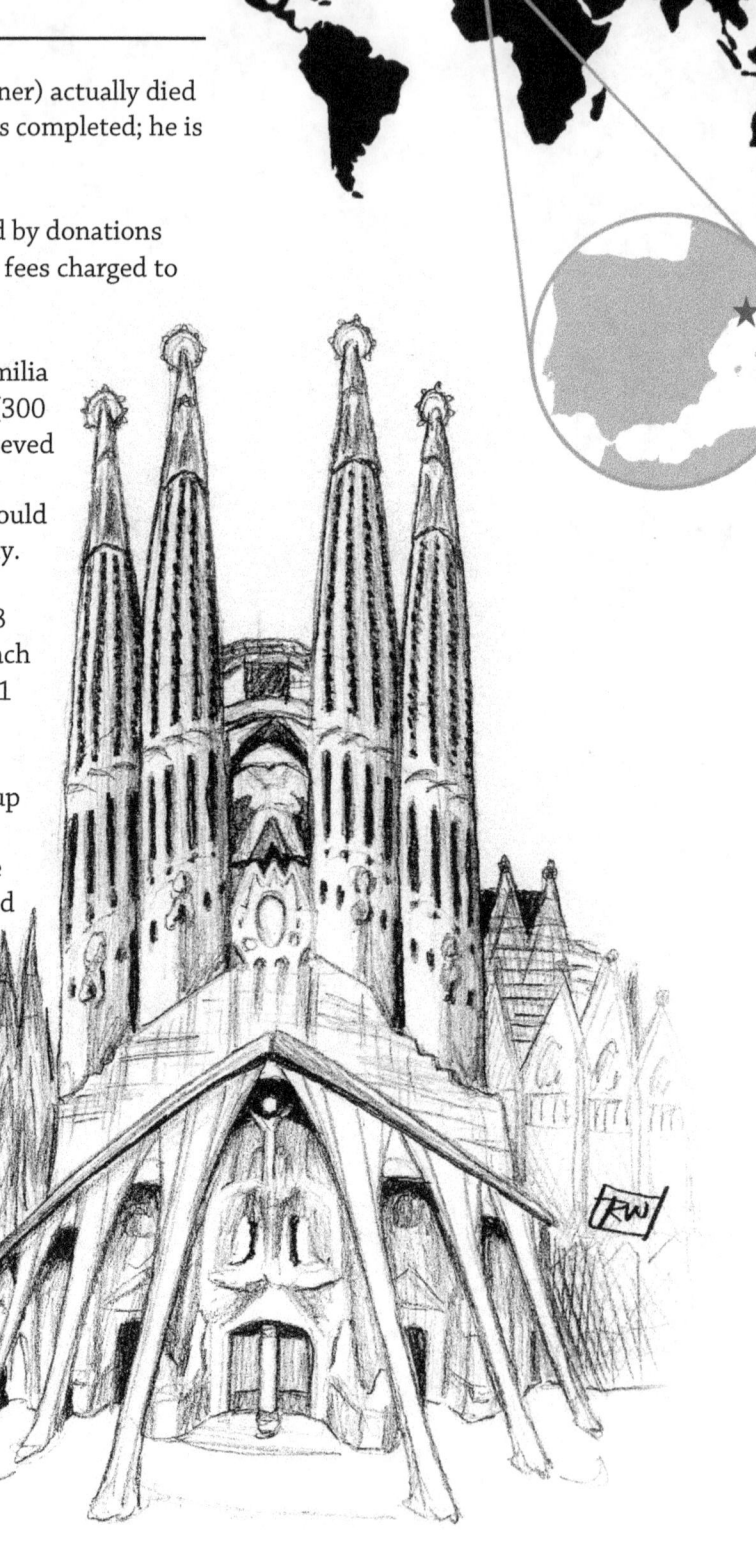

- Antoni Gaudi (architect and designer) actually died before a quarter of the project was completed; he is now buried in the crypt.

- The construction is strictly funded by donations of patrons, as well as the entrance fees charged to view the basilica.

- Per Gaudi's design, La Sagrada Familia will not to be taller than 984 feet (300 meters) above sea level. Gaudi believed the naturally made mountain of Montjuic, standing at 984 feet, should remain the highest point in the city.

- The finished structure will have 18 spires: 12 for each apostle, 4 for each evangelist, 1 for Virgin Mary, and 1 for Jesus Christ.

- It is said that Gaudi did not draw up specific plans for the design of the basilica. Instead, his sketches were frequently changing as he preferred to work organically and modify as construction evolved.

TIP:

Don't be afraid to make your shadows true black.
Keep a piece of black paper nearby as a reference point for how dark you can truly make shadows.

Sahara Desert

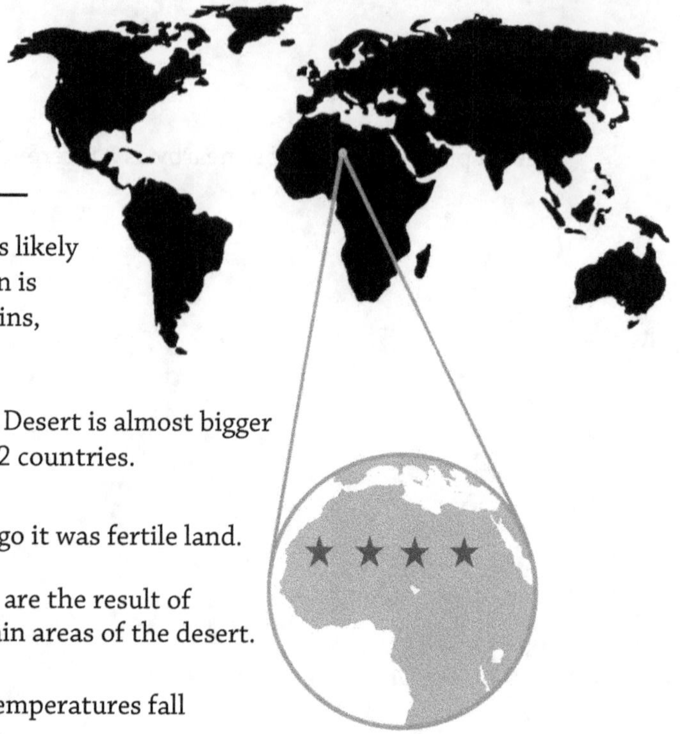

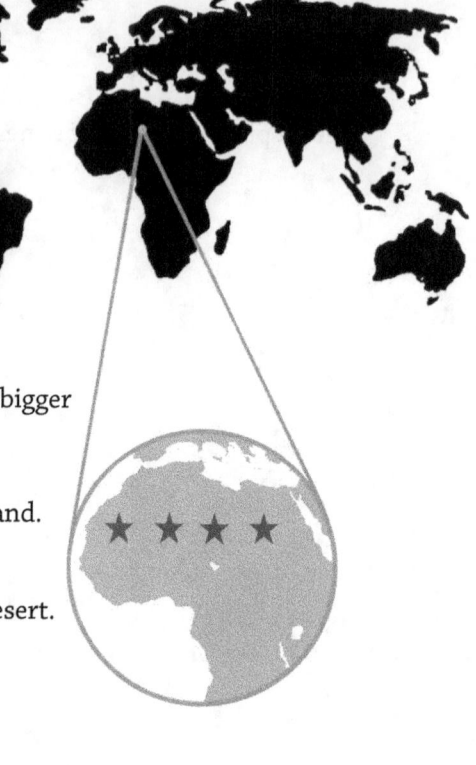

- When you think of the desert your first thought is likely of a vast area of sand. However, the Sahara terrain is quite varied with sand dunes, salt flats, gravel plains, volcanic rock, and dried valleys.

- The amount of land that is covered by the Sahara Desert is almost bigger than the United States of America, and touches 12 countries.

- The Sahara was not always a desert; 8,000 years ago it was fertile land.

- About 2% of its surface is covered by oasis, which are the result of underground rivers coming to the surface in certain areas of the desert.

- It is the world's hottest desert by day, but night temperatures fall to freezing and below, due to the lack of humidity.

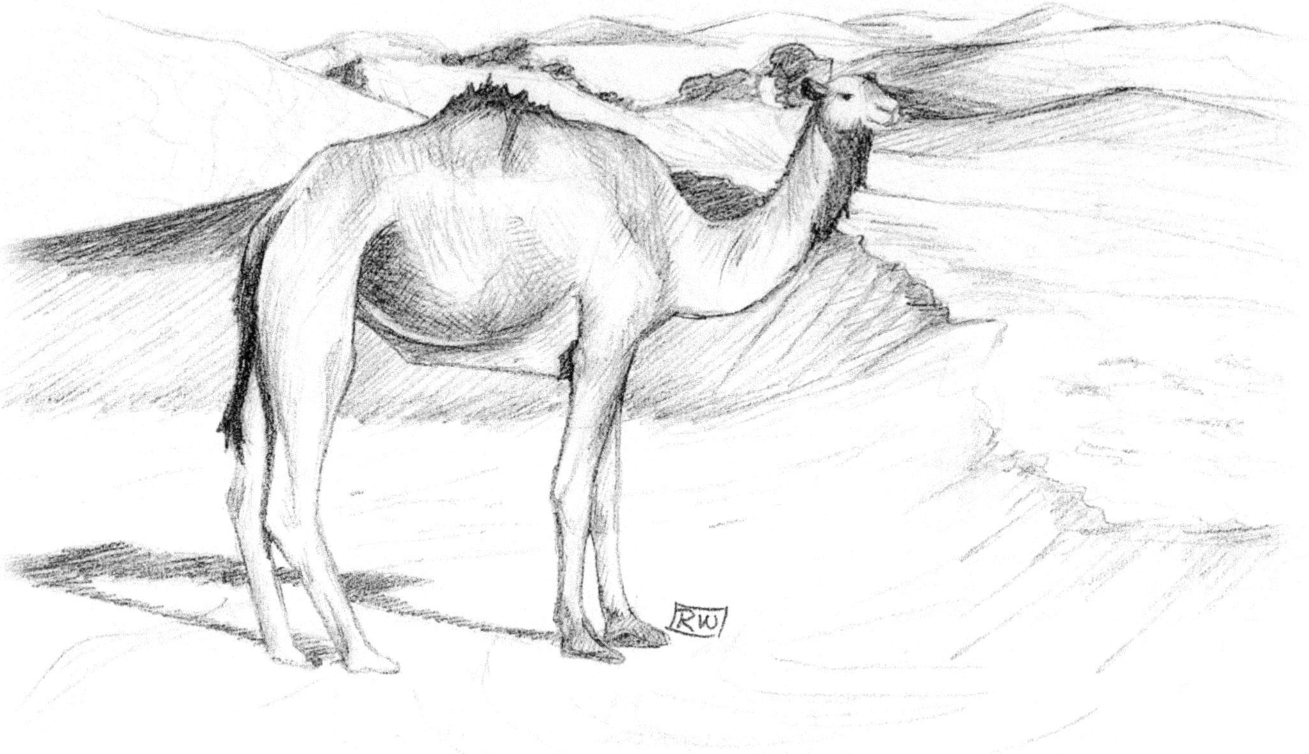

TIP:
Look at the natural contours of the animal's body.
When adding fur or hair, make sure it is sketched in the direction of that countour.

Saint Basil's Cathedral

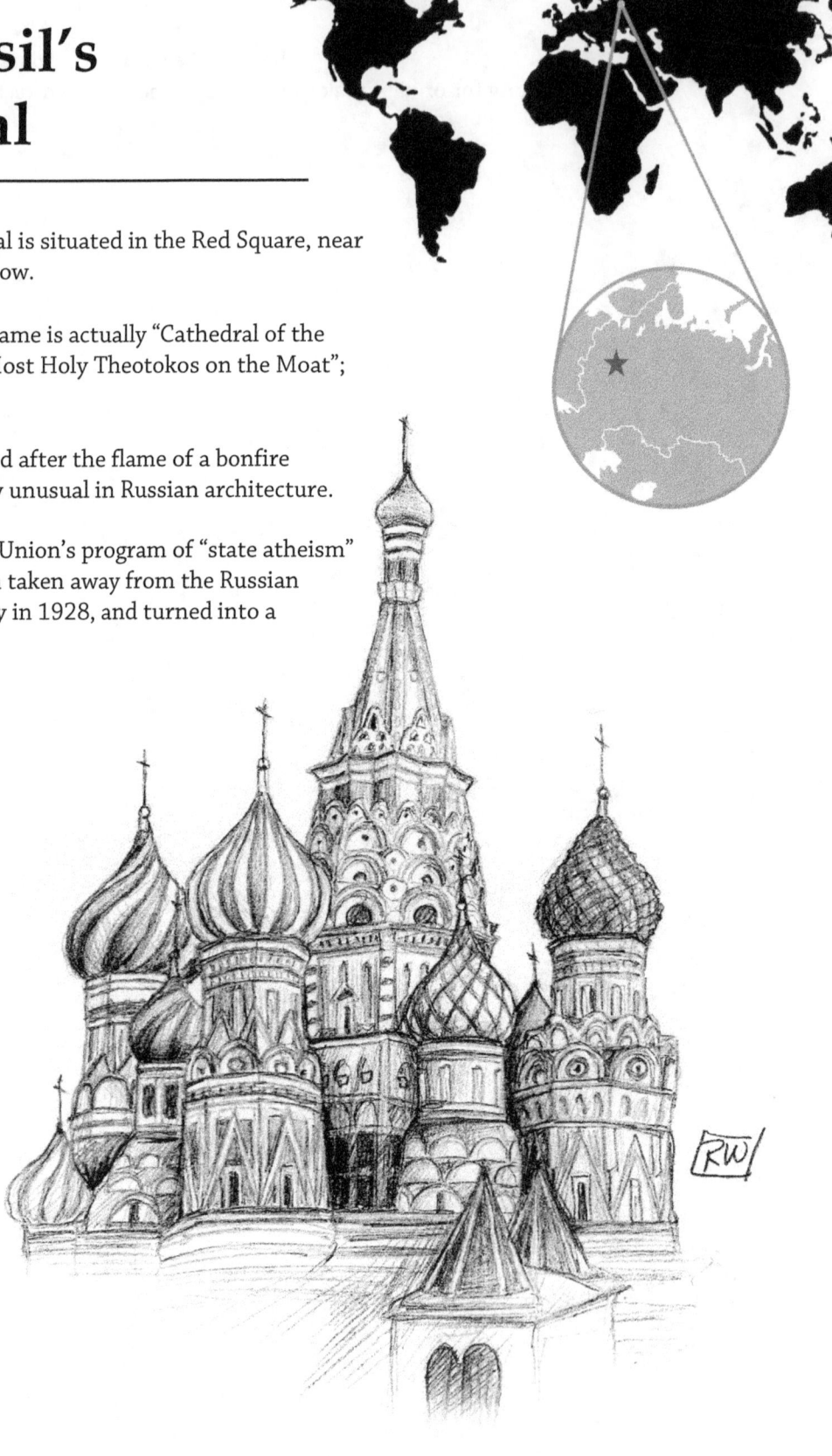

- Saint Basil's Cathedral is situated in the Red Square, near the Kremlin, in Moscow.

- The cathedral's full name is actually "Cathedral of the Intercession of the Most Holy Theotokos on the Moat"; what a mouthful!

- The building is shaped after the flame of a bonfire rising to the sky; very unusual in Russian architecture.

- As part of the Soviet Union's program of "state atheism" the building has been taken away from the Russian Orthodox community in 1928, and turned into a museum.

Saint Peter's Basilica

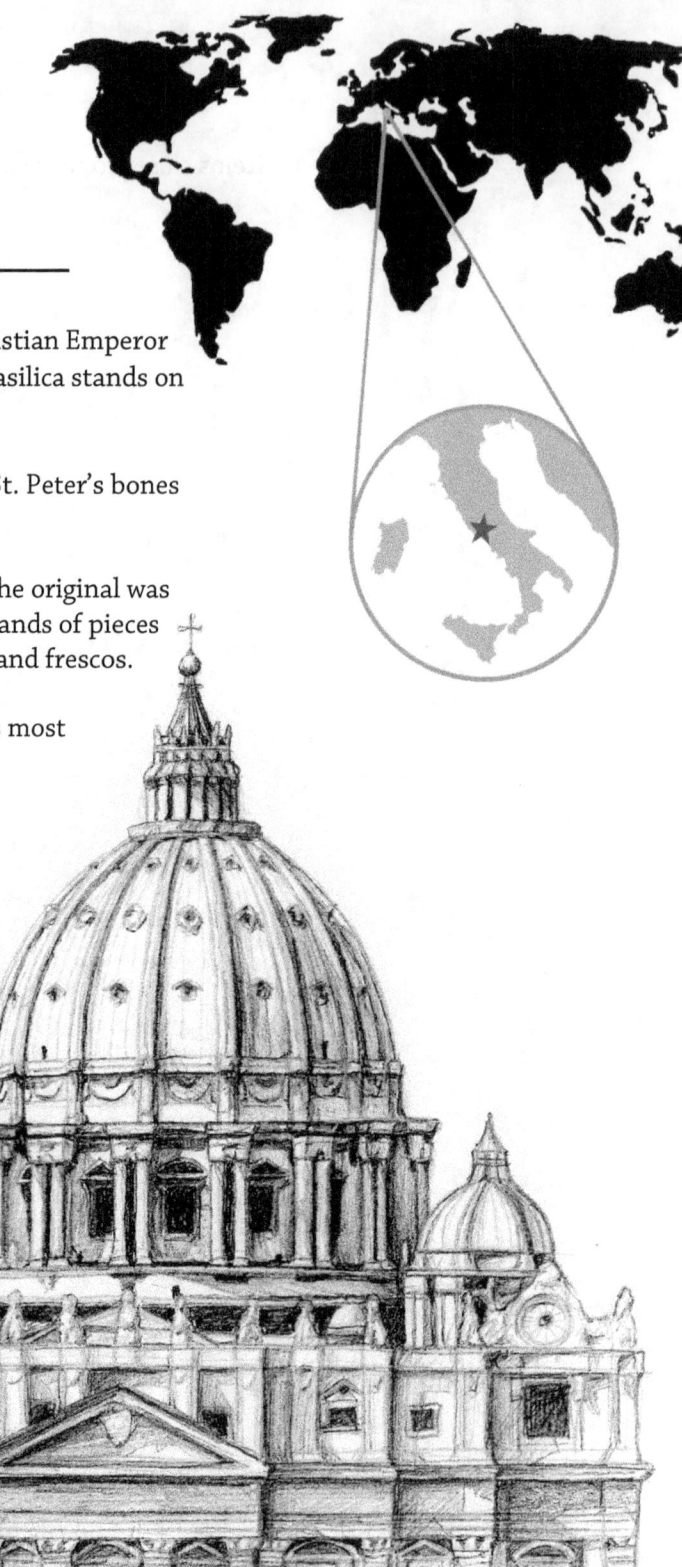

- The original basilica was built by the first Christian Emperor Constantine in the 4th century. The current basilica stands on the same location.

- The altar was placed over the location where St. Peter's bones were thought to lay.

- The current basilica is the second structure. The original was torn down by Pope Julius II, destroying thousands of pieces of priceless artwork such as statues, mosaics, and frescos.

- This is also the home to one of Michelangelo's most famous masterpieces, the *Pietà*.

- St. Peter's Basilica is neither a cathedral, nor the seat of the Pope. However, due to its proximity to the Pope's residence, it is where the majority of religious ceremonies take place.

TIP:

When your sketch is close to completion, use a heavy outline to finalize the drawing.

Santorini, Greece

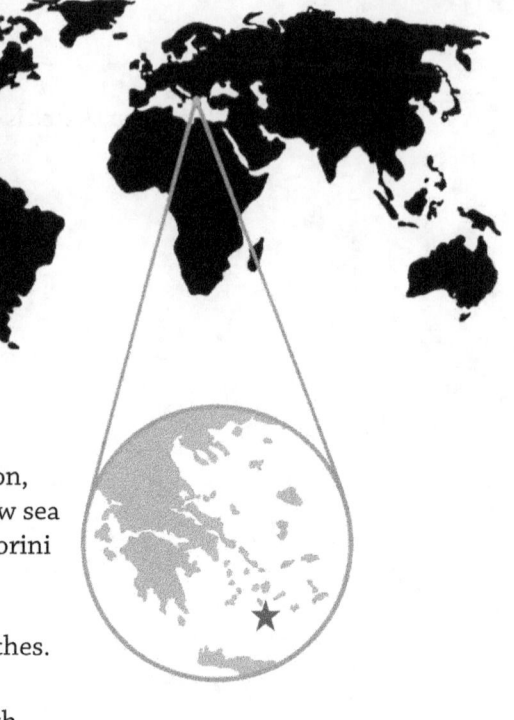

- Santorini is one of the most famous and beautiful islands in Greece and a popular tourist destination.

- It was formed out of the lava from a volcanic eruption in 1660 BC, which is thought to have also ended the Minoan civilization in Crete.

- Santorini was once a round island, but after the volcanic eruption, the central part of the volcano (known as the caldera) sank below sea level causing a giant hole in the middle of the island. Now, Santorini is more like a ring of small islands.

- Due to its volcanic past, Santorini has white, black, and red beaches.

- The volcano is registered as one of the most active in Greece with over 12 explosive eruptions over its lifetime.

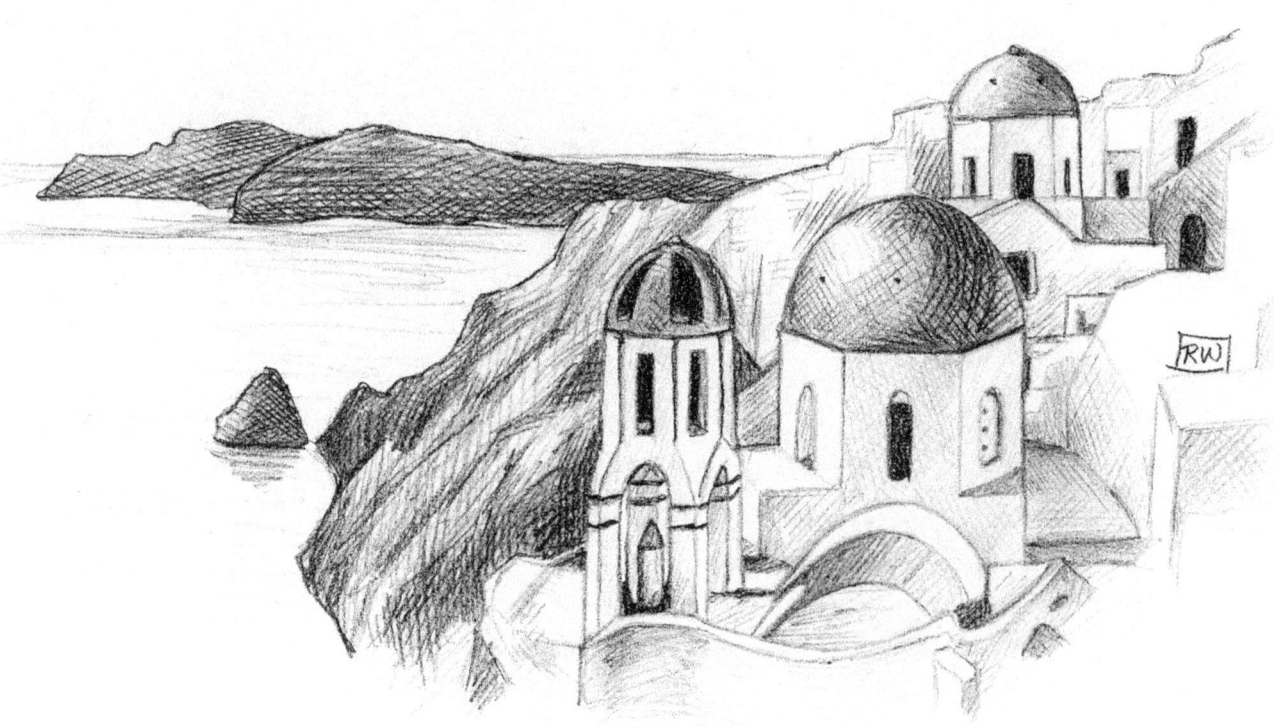

TIP:

When sketching round objects, feel free to trace a physical item with the same size to get the shape you want. A protractor and compass can also be used to get perfect circles.

Shitennō-ji Temple

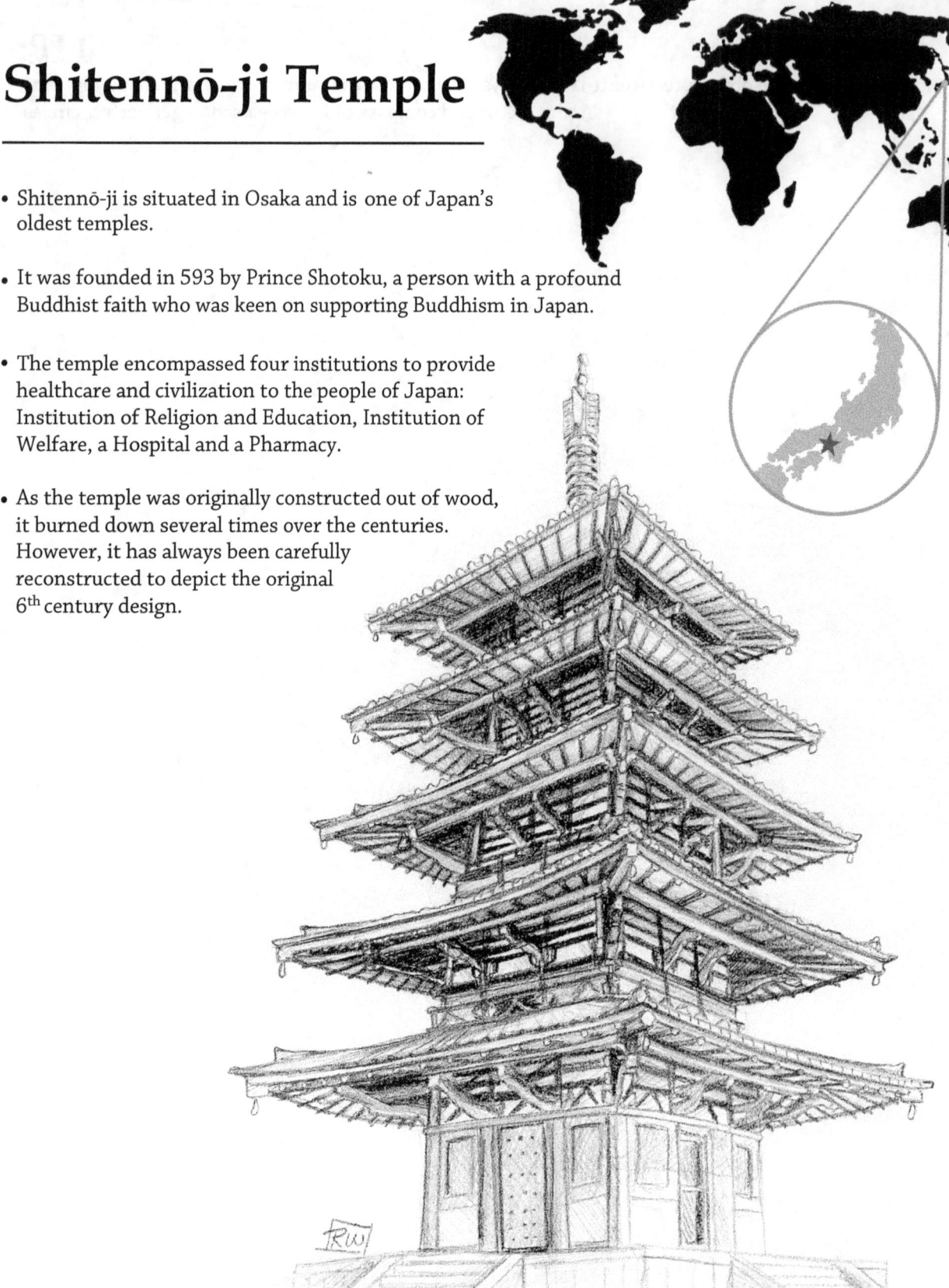

- Shitennō-ji is situated in Osaka and is one of Japan's oldest temples.

- It was founded in 593 by Prince Shotoku, a person with a profound Buddhist faith who was keen on supporting Buddhism in Japan.

- The temple encompassed four institutions to provide healthcare and civilization to the people of Japan: Institution of Religion and Education, Institution of Welfare, a Hospital and a Pharmacy.

- As the temple was originally constructed out of wood, it burned down several times over the centuries. However, it has always been carefully reconstructed to depict the original 6th century design.

TIP:

Sometimes it's easier to use a darker pencil first, to darken in the deepest shadows.

Souks of Marrakech

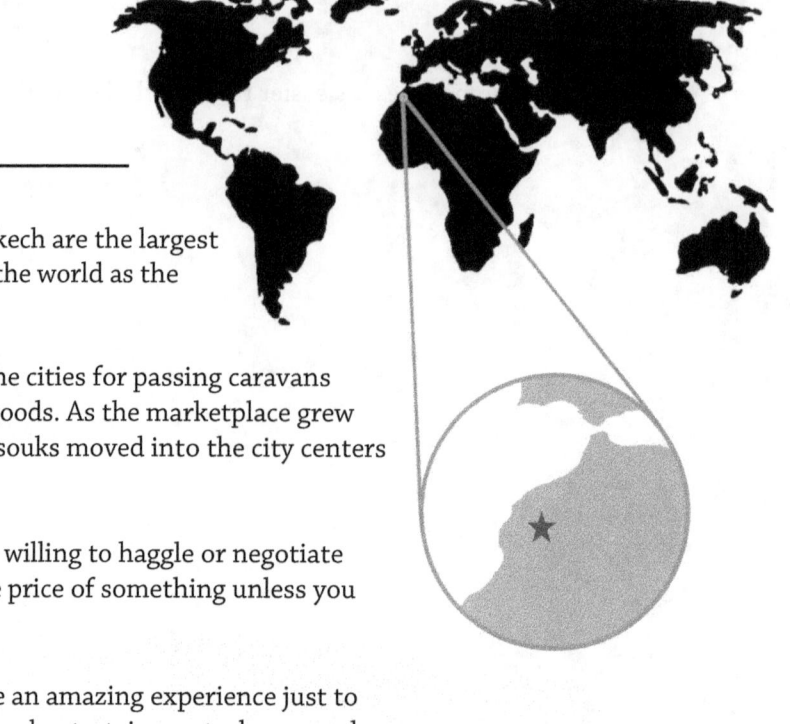

- The souks, "open air markets", in Marrakech are the largest in Morocco, and are known throughout the world as the most exotic place to shop.

- Souks were historically held outside of the cities for passing caravans and merchants to display and sell their goods. As the marketplace grew more important in developed cities, the souks moved into the city centers to accommodate city growth.

- The majority of vendors in the souks are willing to haggle or negotiate price. However, it is ill advised to ask the price of something unless you truly intend to purchase.

- If you aren't into shopping, the souks are an amazing experience just to walk through for bragging rights; additional entertainment, shows, and snake charmers can be found in the souks as well.

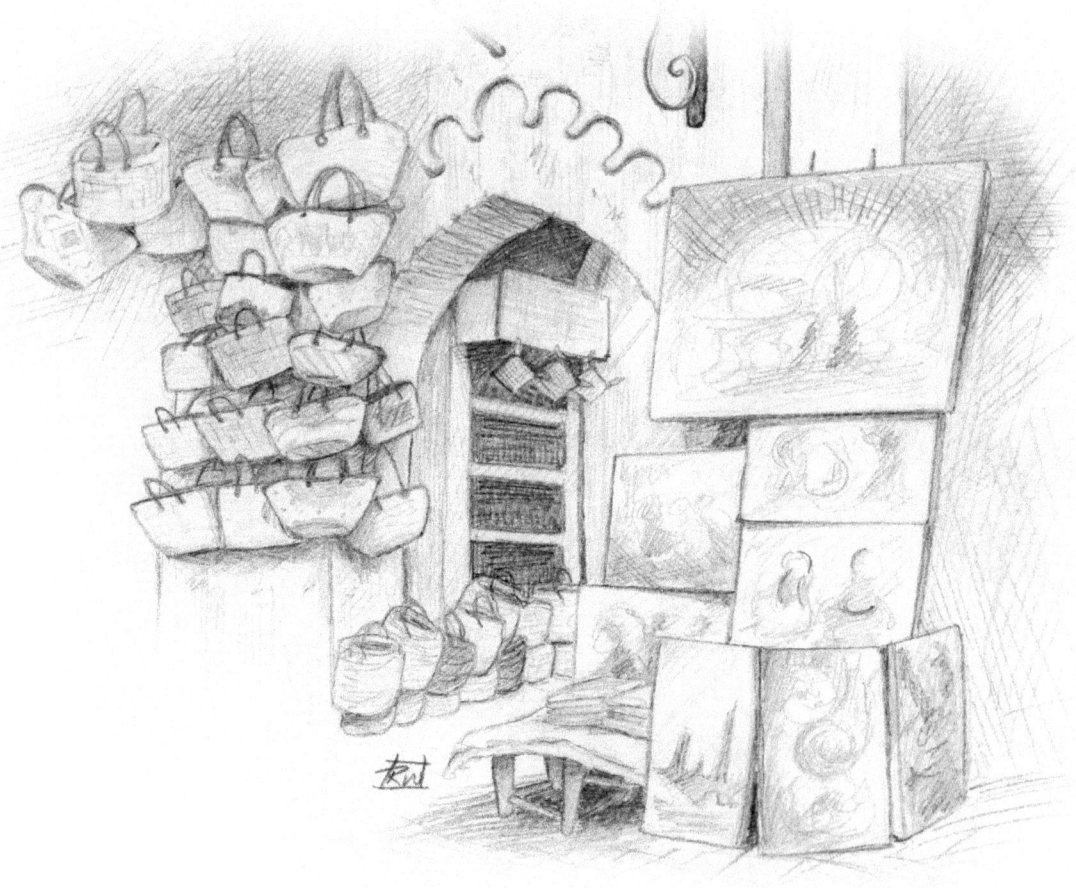

TIP:

When drawing a painting within your own sketch, extreme details aren't really necessary.

Spanish Steps

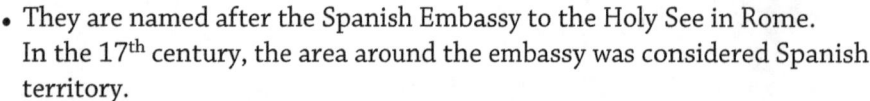

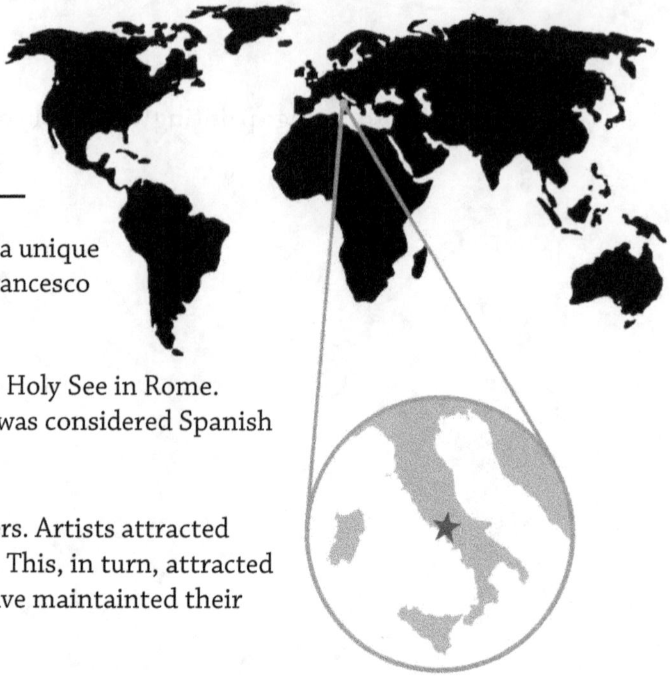

- The Spanish steps were built in 1723 - 1725 with a unique design and elegance by a little-known architect Francesco de Sanctis.

- They are named after the Spanish Embassy to the Holy See in Rome. In the 17th century, the area around the embassy was considered Spanish territory.

- It used to be a popular place for artists and painters. Artists attracted beautiful women with hopes of becoming models. This, in turn, attracted rich Romans and visitors. Since then, the steps have maintainted their reputation as a meeting place.

- A statue known as the *Barcaccia* (old boat) sits at the foot of the steps and stands as a remembrance to the flood of the Tiber River in 1598; it is said a fishing boat landed at the location of the current fountain.

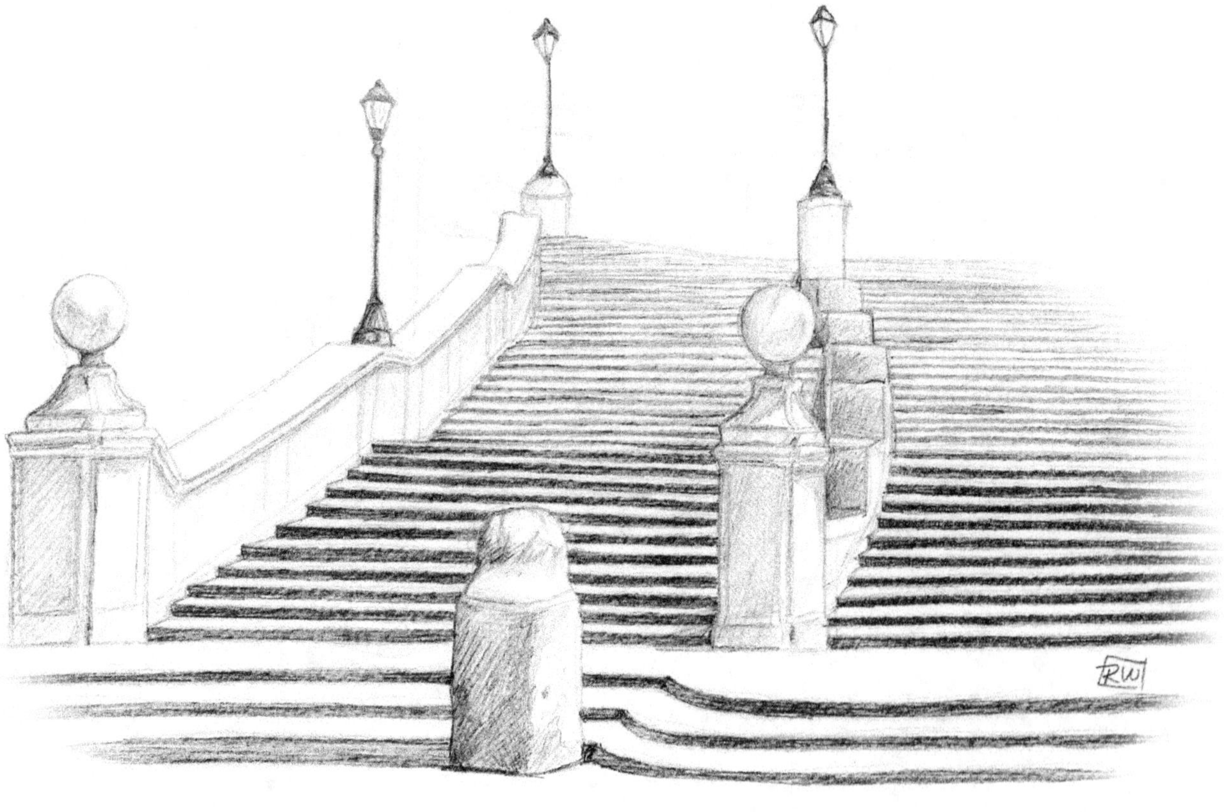

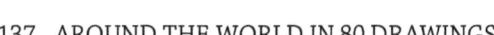

TIP:
Practice makes perfect.
Repeated shapes throughout a sketch are a good way to perfect a technique.

Statue of Liberty

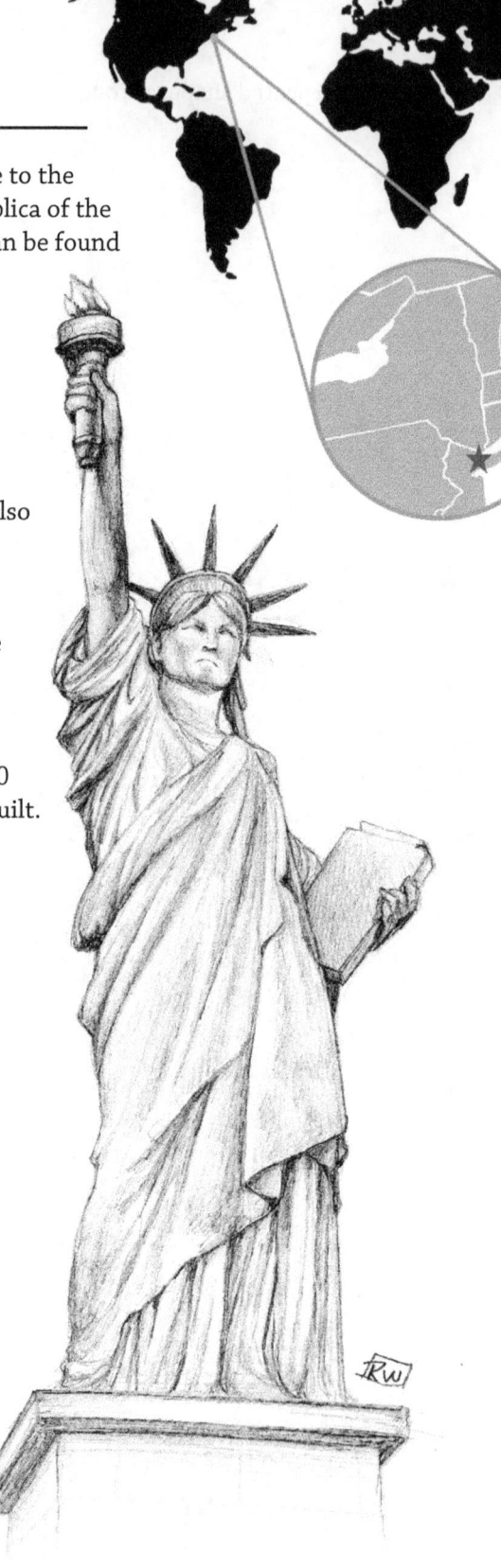

- The Statue of Liberty was a gift from France to the United States in 1886. However, she is a replica of the original statue which is more life size and can be found in the Jardin de Luxembourg, in Paris.

- She holds a tablet inscribed with the date July 4, 1776; the date of the American Declaration of Independence.

- She has a copper exterior, which has turned green due to oxidation. This green coating also acts as a form of protection, from age and weather.

- The seven spikes of her crown represent the seven oceans and seven continents of the world; a global representation of liberty.

- The statue is said to be struck by around 600 bolts of lightning every year since she was built.

Stonehenge

- Stonehenge is a prehistoric monument made of a ring of huge, standing stones. It was built in England between 3000 BC and 2000 BC, by Neolithic people without any engineering knowledge.

- There are different theories about the purpose of Stonehenge. Some say it was used for burials, human sacrifices, or religious worship. Others believe it was built by the wizard Merlin or aliens.

- Some researchers suggest Stonehenge sits at its current location because it aligned with the important solar events of the summer and winter solstices.

- A replica of Stonehenge is built in Nebraska, USA constructed using old, vintage cars as a modern form of "Car Art"; it's called "Carhenge".

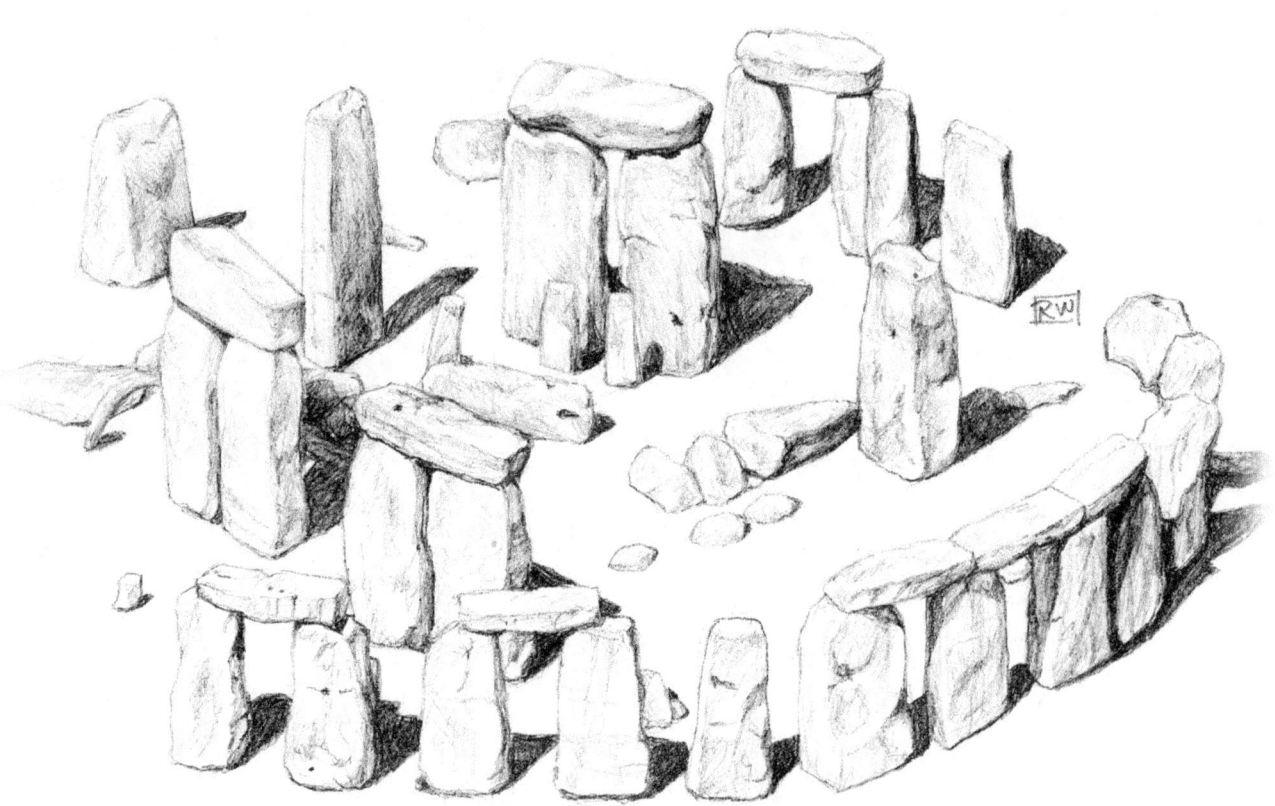

Sydney Opera House

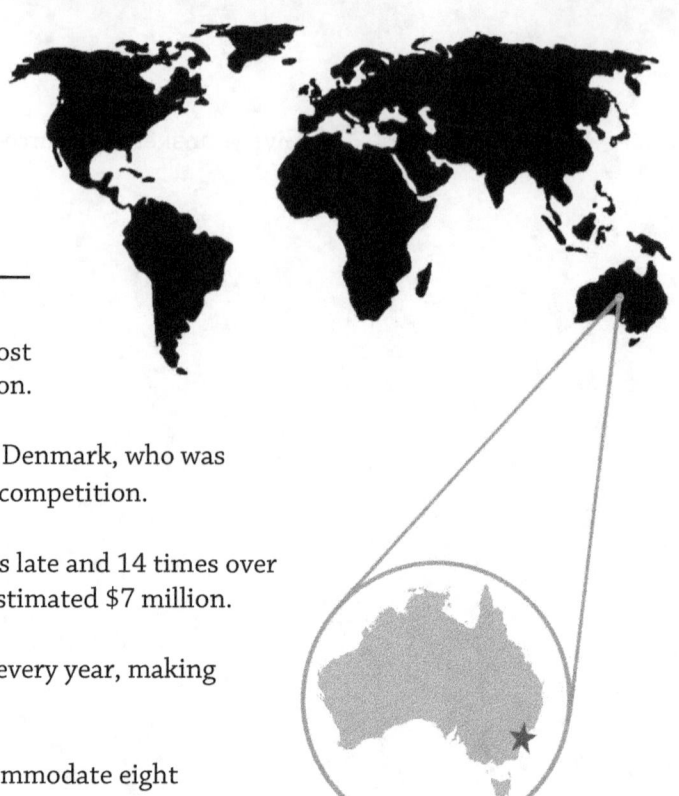

- The Sydney Opera House is one of the world's most well-known music venues, and is an Australian icon.

- It was designed by Jorn Utzon, an architect from Denmark, who was selected as the winner of an international design competition.

- The construction was completed in 1973, 10 years late and 14 times over budget; it cost $102 million AUD instead of the estimated $7 million.

- Over seven million people visit the Opera House every year, making it one of Australia's biggest tourist attractions.

- The site of the Opera House is so large it can accommodate eight Boeing-747 airplanes wing-to-wing!

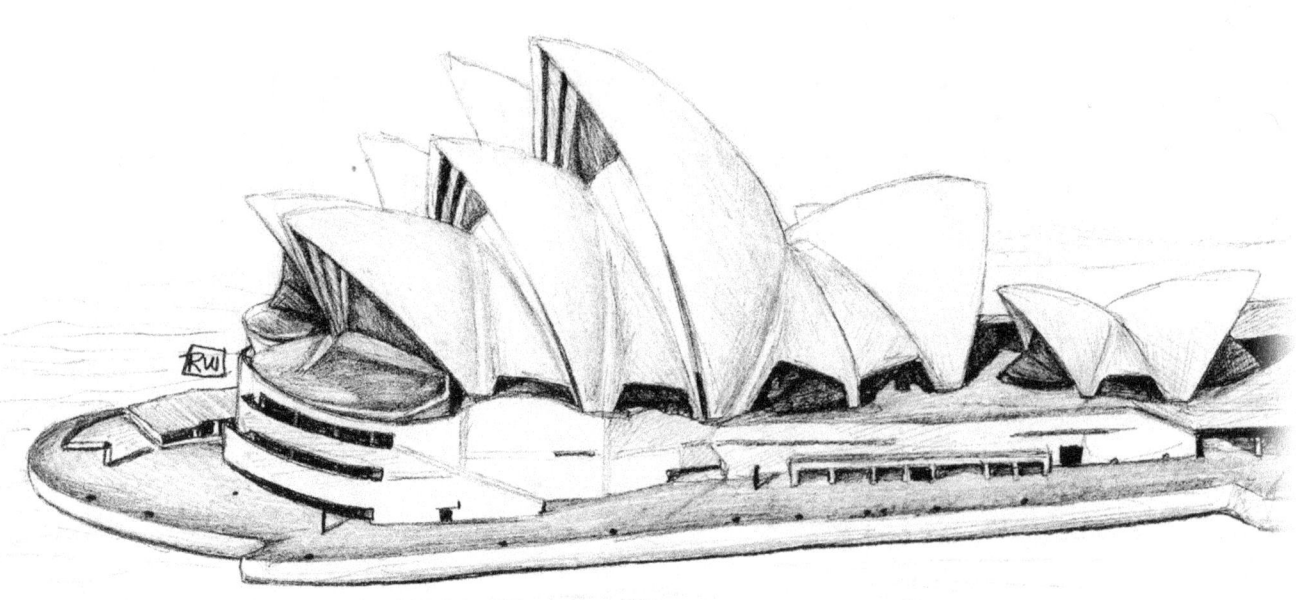

Simple shading gives the smoothest looking quality to the sketch's surface.
Use lower numbered pencils for darker tones.

Table Mountain

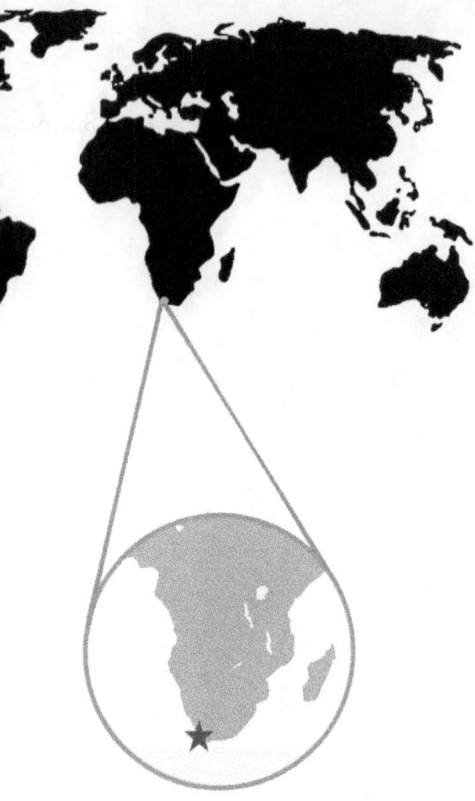

- Table Mountain overlooks Cape Town, in South Africa. It was given its name due to its main feature: the flat level plateau on top.

- The top of the mountain is often covered in clouds, which forms the so called "table-cloth".

- It is thought to be one of the oldest mountains in the world. Table Mountain is much older than the Andes, Rockies, Himalayas or the Alps.

- There are around 2,200 species of plant life that are indigenous to the mountain and cannot be found anywhere else in the world.

- It is possible to hike to the top of Table Mountain. However, if you choose not to hike, there is a cable car that will take you to the top. Once at the summit, you can appreciate spectacular views of the city of Cape Town.

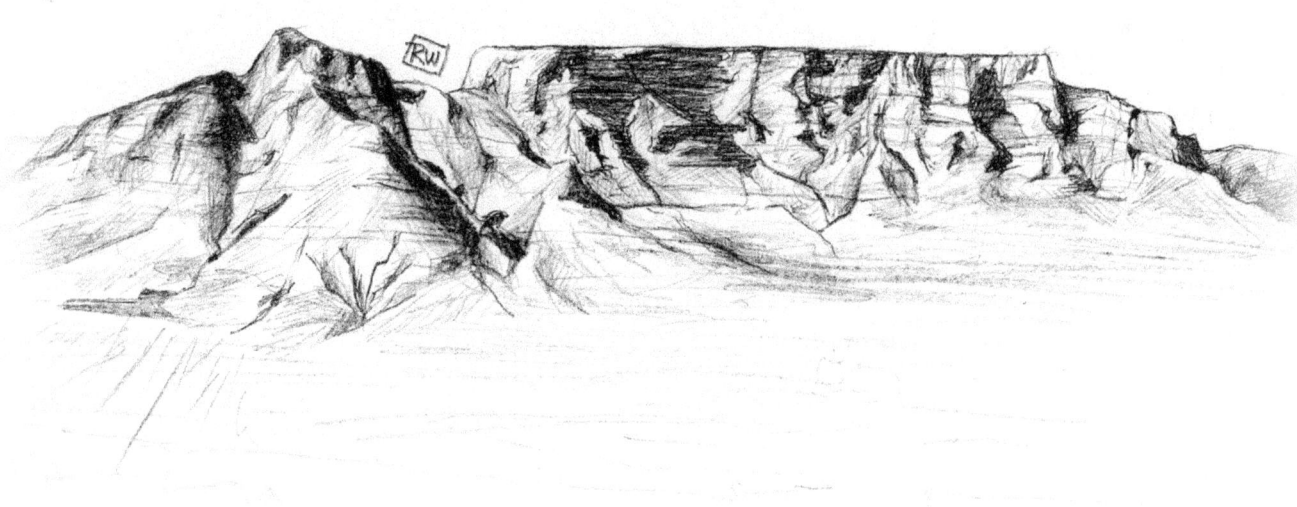

Block shading, or using flat shades for solid areas, is sometimes best to sketch certain forms.

Taj Mahal

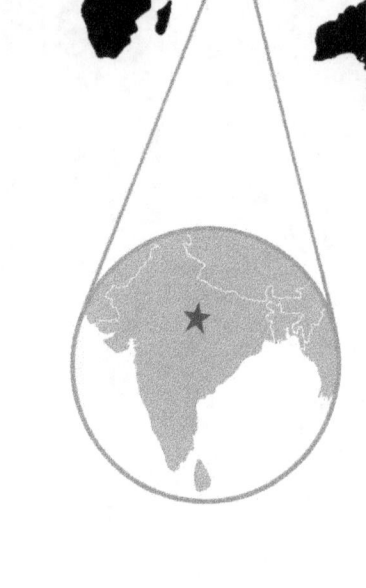

- The Taj Mahal is a white marble mausoleum in the city of Agra, in northern India.

- The name means "crown of palaces".

- It was built by Emperor Shah Jahan in 1632 in memory of his wife, Mumtaz Mahal, who died during the birth of their 14th child.

- There is a myth that the Taj Mahal would actually have a twin constructed out of black marble, built on the opposite side of the Yamuna River. This was rumored to serve as the future mausoleum for the Shah Jahan.

- It combines elements of Islamic, Persian, Ottoman Turkish and Indian architectural styles.

- The Taj Mahal's most famous feature is the large dome that is often called the "onion dome" due to its shape.

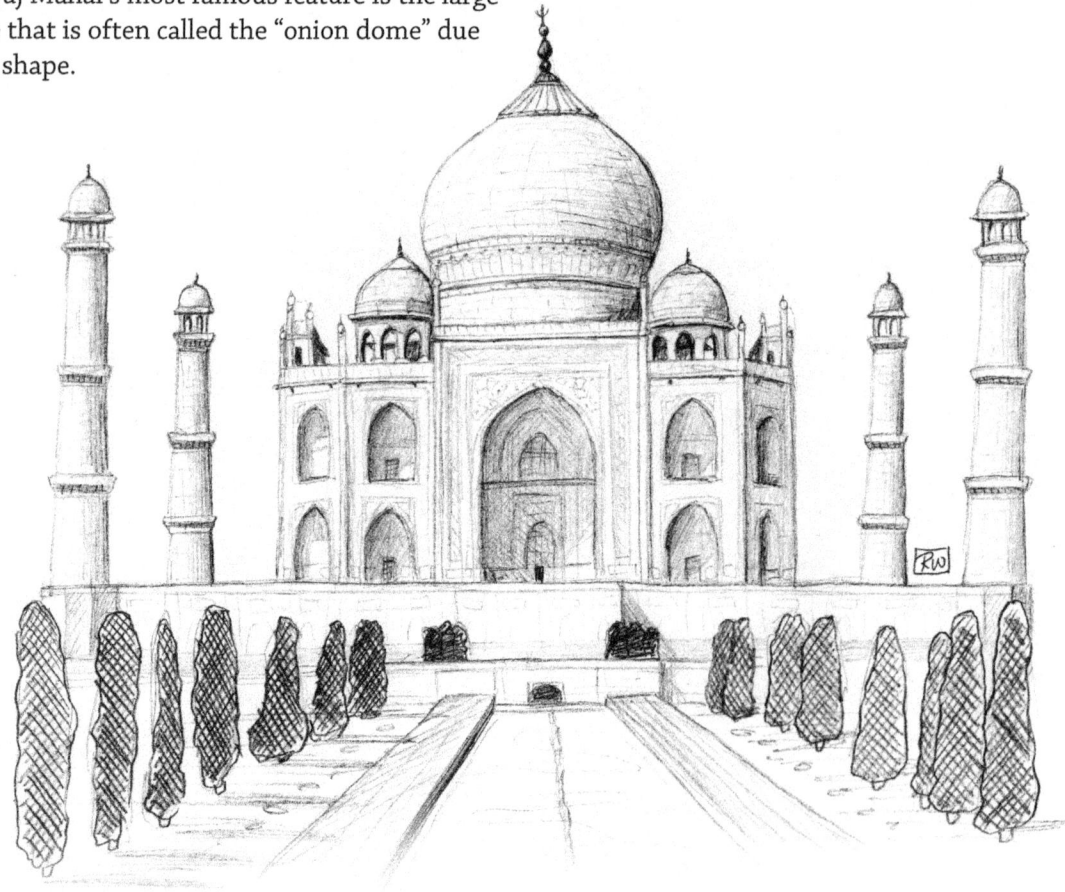

TIP:
You don't always have to draw reflections in water.
It's not always necessary and can sometimes cause a loss of focus.

Temple of the Emerald Buddha

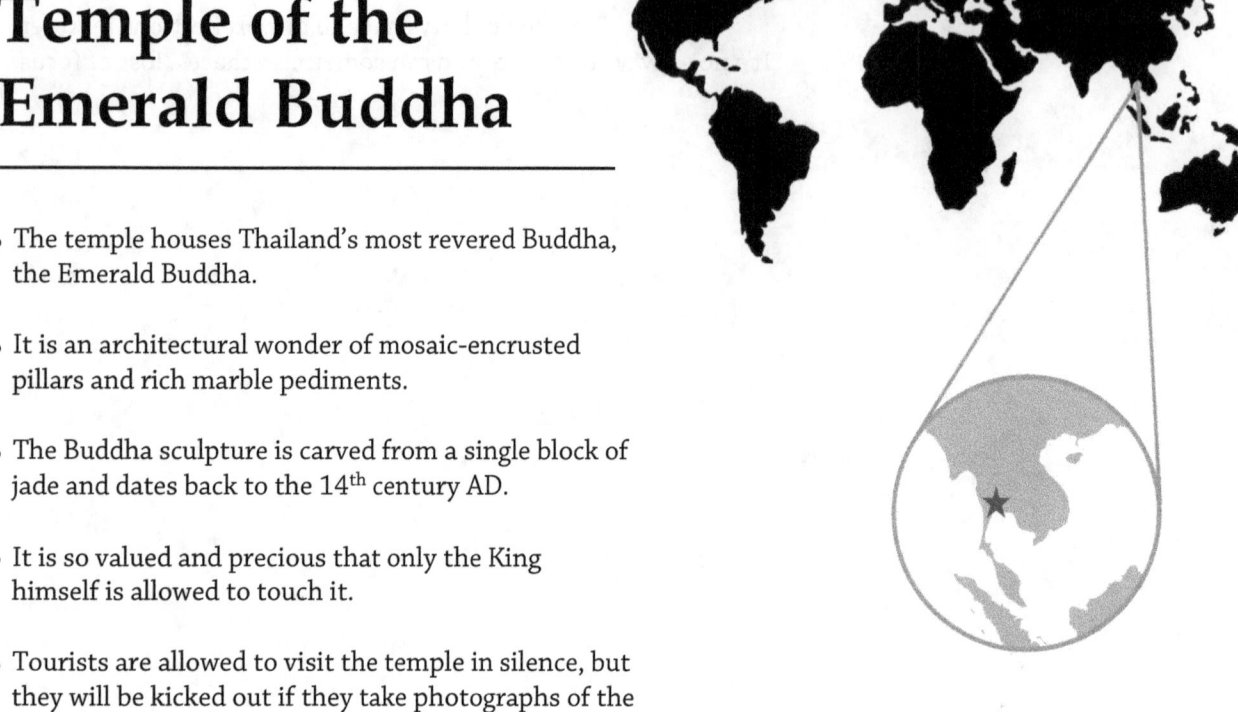

- The temple houses Thailand's most revered Buddha, the Emerald Buddha.

- It is an architectural wonder of mosaic-encrusted pillars and rich marble pediments.

- The Buddha sculpture is carved from a single block of jade and dates back to the 14th century AD.

- It is so valued and precious that only the King himself is allowed to touch it.

- Tourists are allowed to visit the temple in silence, but they will be kicked out if they take photographs of the sculpture or if they sit pointing their feet at it.

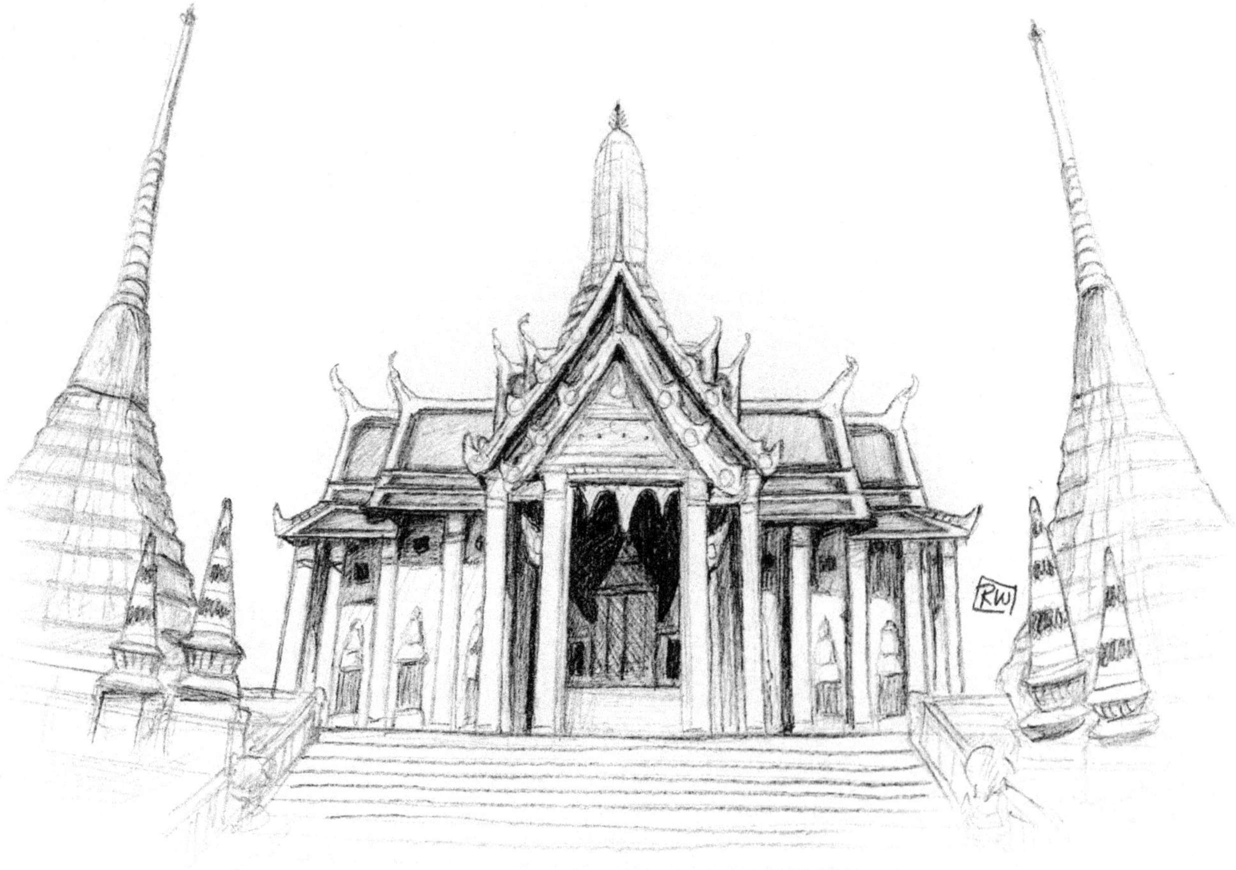

A well placed window or doorway with dark shading can be a great focus point in a sketch.

Temple of Poseidon

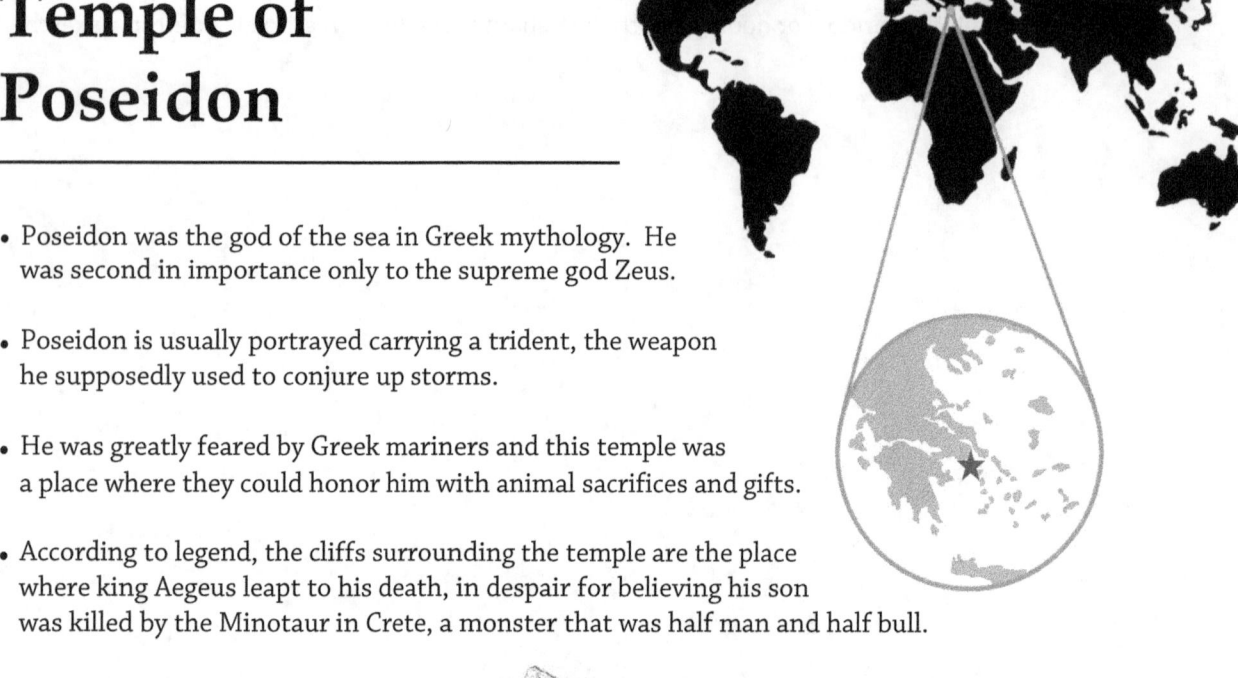

- Poseidon was the god of the sea in Greek mythology. He was second in importance only to the supreme god Zeus.

- Poseidon is usually portrayed carrying a trident, the weapon he supposedly used to conjure up storms.

- He was greatly feared by Greek mariners and this temple was a place where they could honor him with animal sacrifices and gifts.

- According to legend, the cliffs surrounding the temple are the place where king Aegeus leapt to his death, in despair for believing his son was killed by the Minotaur in Crete, a monster that was half man and half bull.

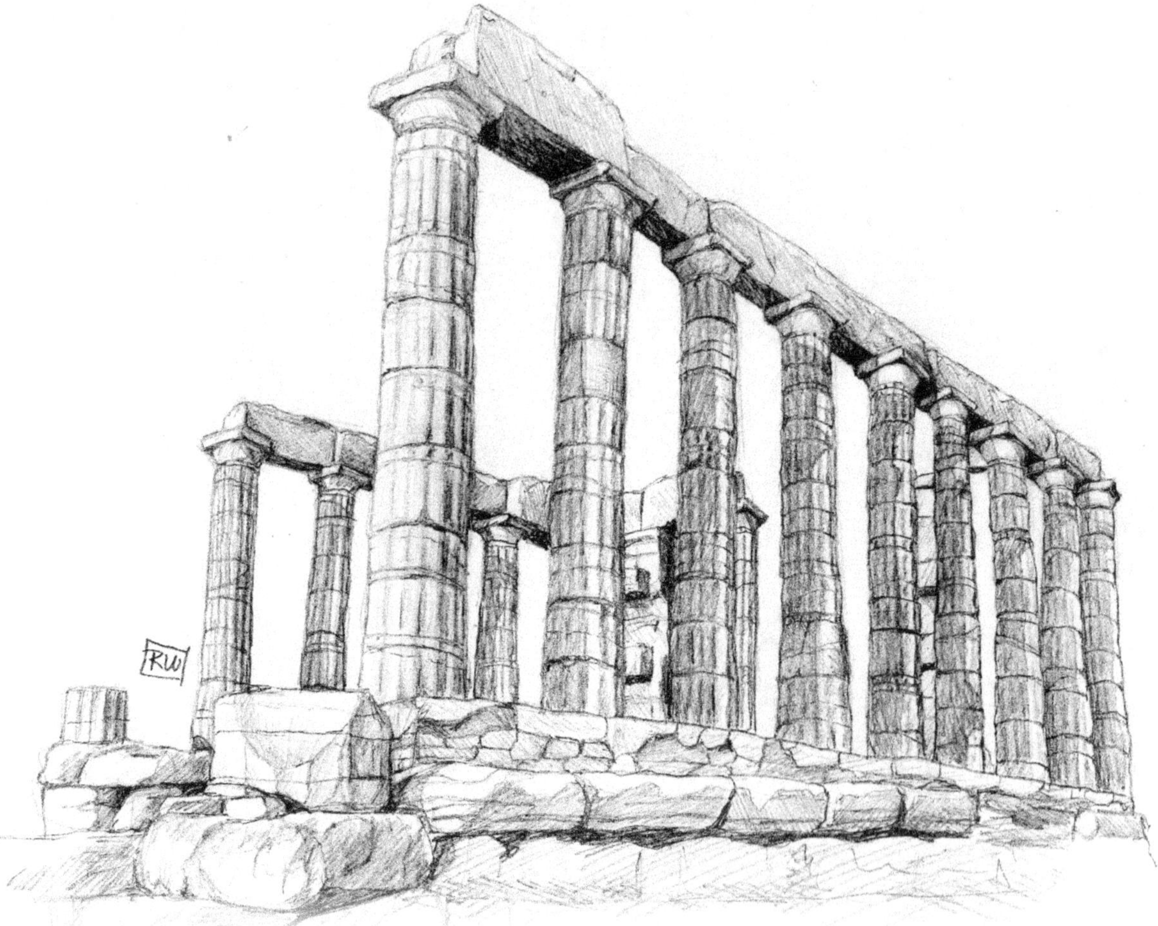

The use of various shades, contrasts and textures will give a realistic appearance to stone.

Times Square

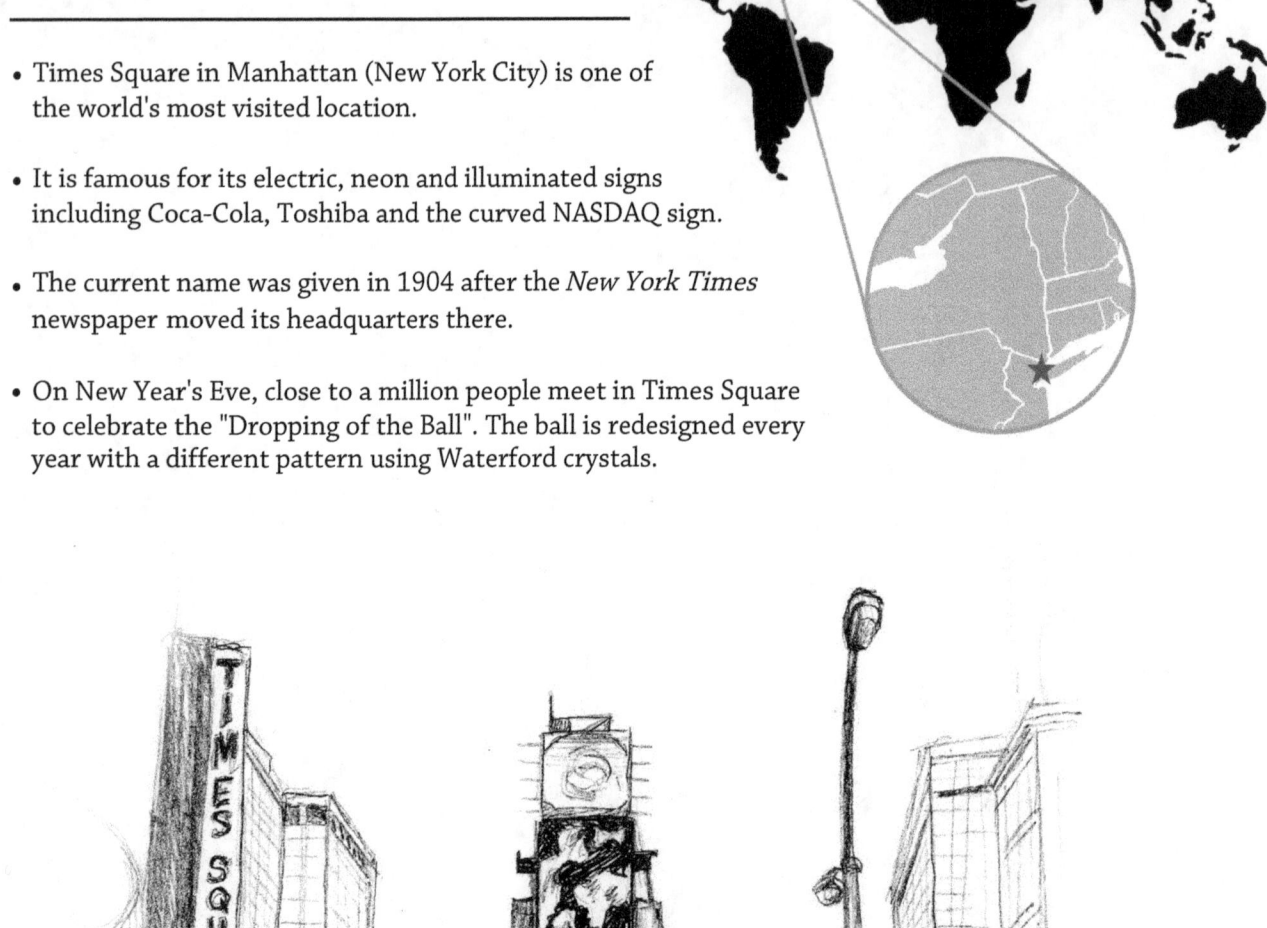

- Times Square in Manhattan (New York City) is one of the world's most visited location.

- It is famous for its electric, neon and illuminated signs including Coca-Cola, Toshiba and the curved NASDAQ sign.

- The current name was given in 1904 after the *New York Times* newspaper moved its headquarters there.

- On New Year's Eve, close to a million people meet in Times Square to celebrate the "Dropping of the Ball". The ball is redesigned every year with a different pattern using Waterford crystals.

TIP:

Just because buildings have straight lines, don't feel the need to always use a ruler. Sometimes it's okay to freehand sketch.

Tower Bridge

- This bridge is an iconic symbol of London and was officially opened in 1894. Many people actually mistake Tower Bridge, for London Bridge.

- River traffic takes priority over bridge users, in fact, the draw bridge is raised more than 1,000 times a year!

- Construction took 8 years, 70,000 tons of concrete and 11,000 tons of steel.

- In 1952, a London bus had to leap from one side of the bridge to the other when the bridge began to rise with the #78 bus still on it!

- It is crossed by over 40,000 people every day.

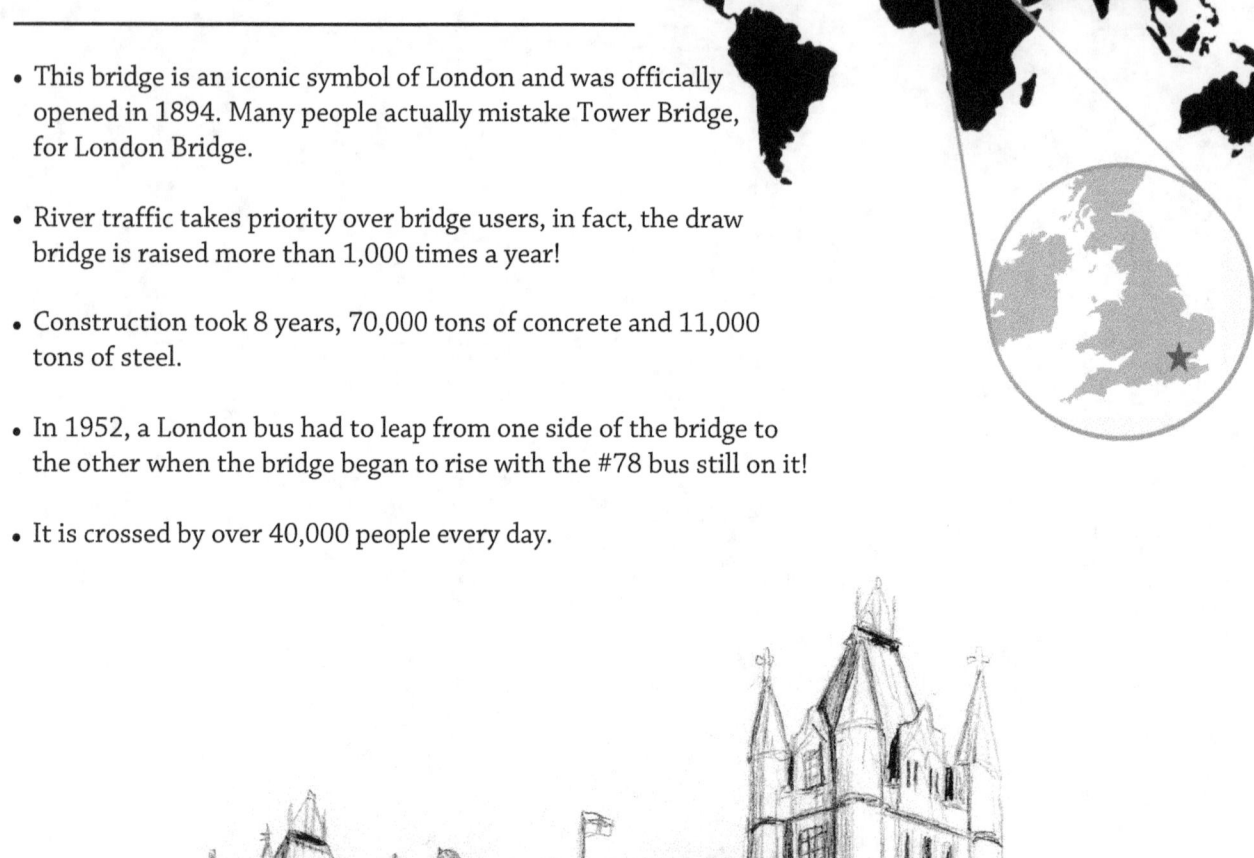

Don't be afraid to go over marks you made earlier to darken them into shadows or distinct lines.

Venice

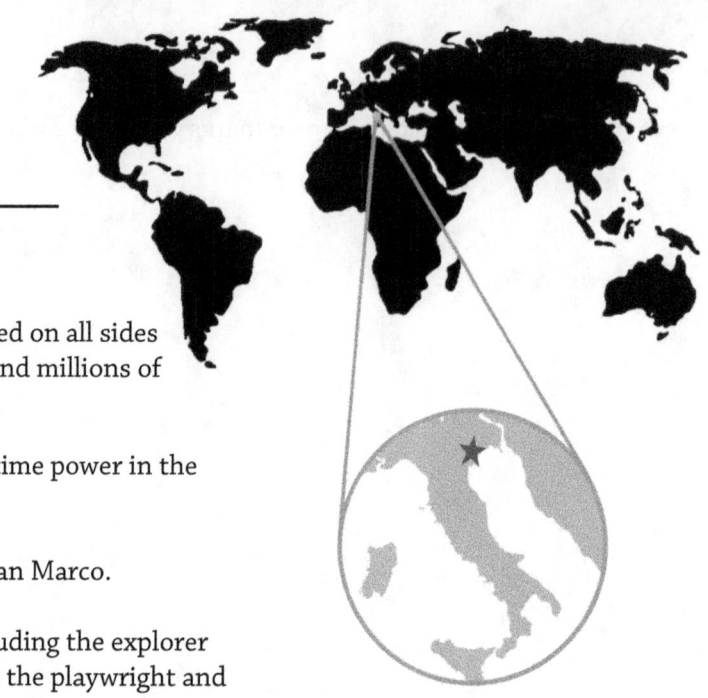

- Venice is sinking 1-2 millimeters a year.

- It is built on 118 submerged islands, surrounded on all sides by water. It has over 400 bridges, 170 canals, and millions of wooden piles that support the city.

- Venice became the major Mediterranean maritime power in the 14th to 16th centuries.

- St. Mark's remains are buried here, in Piazza San Marco.

- Many famous people were born in Venice, including the explorer Marco Polo, the composer Antonio Vivaldi and the playwright and lover Giacomo Casanova.

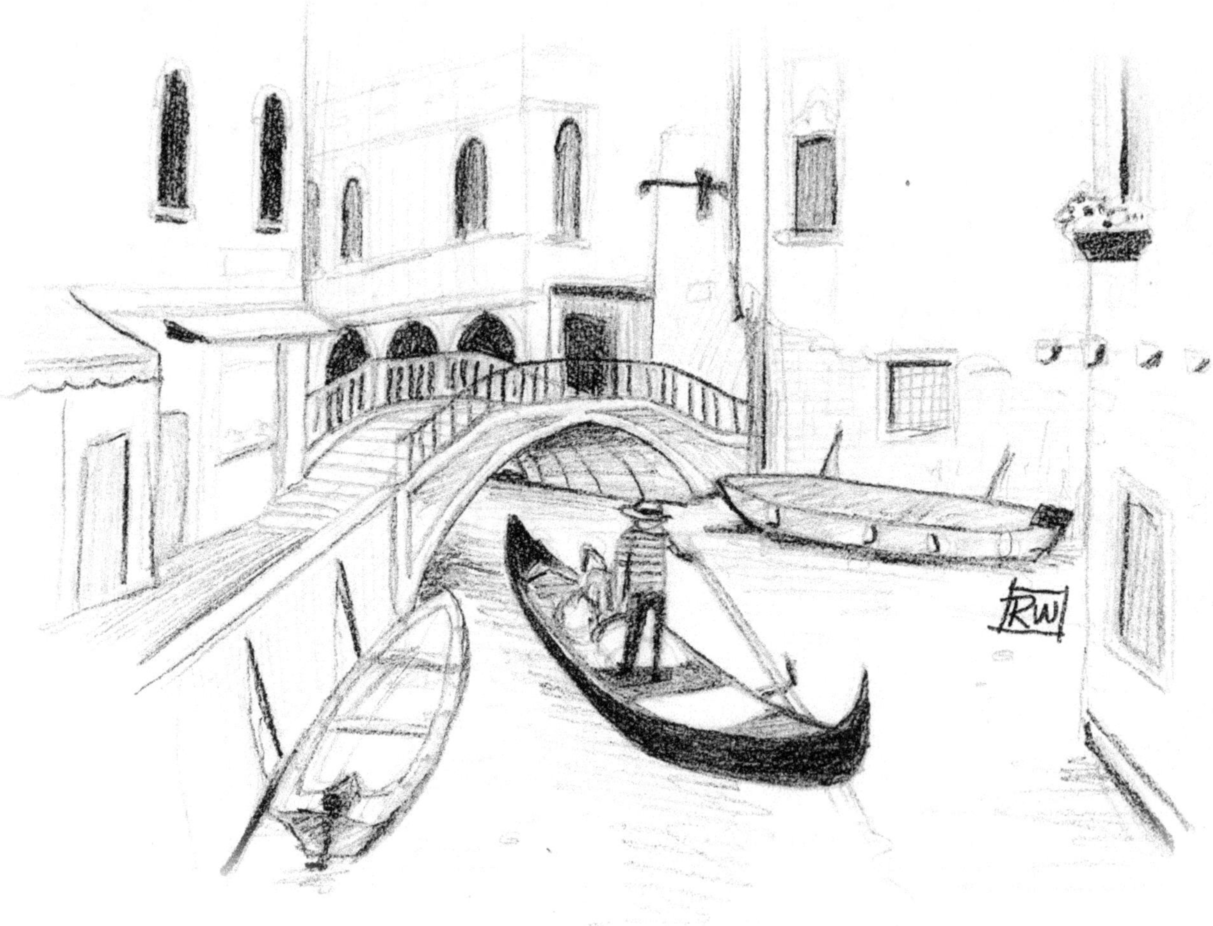

TIP:

Give a sense of scale whenever possible.
Adding a person to show just how big or small a structure or object is.

Windmills of La Mancha

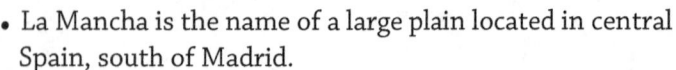

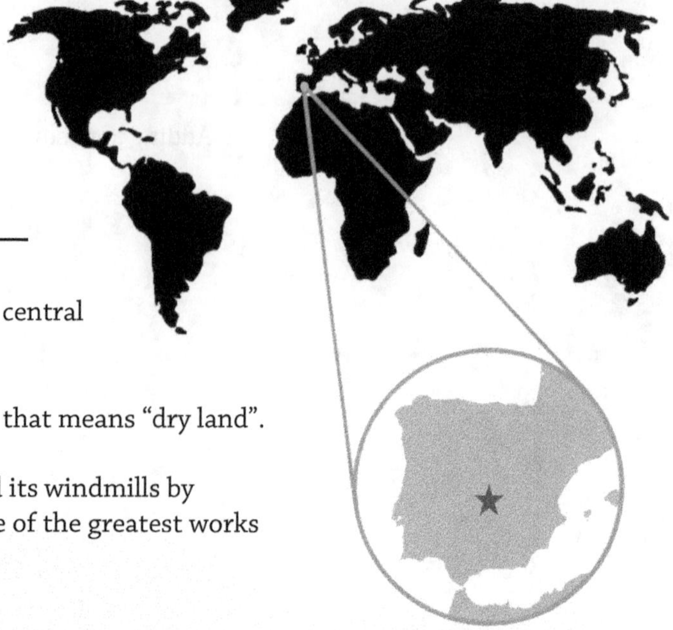

- La Mancha is the name of a large plain located in central Spain, south of Madrid.

- The name is probably derived from an Arab word that means "dry land".

- Miguel de Cervantes gave fame to this region and its windmills by writing the novel *Don Quixote de La Mancha*, one of the greatest works of Spanish literature.

- The story of Don Quixote was published in 1605 and follows the adventures of Alonso Quijano; a 50 year old man from La Mancha who loses his wits and becomes obsessed with books of chivalry. He soon decides to become a knight-errant and travel with a horse and armor in search of adventures.

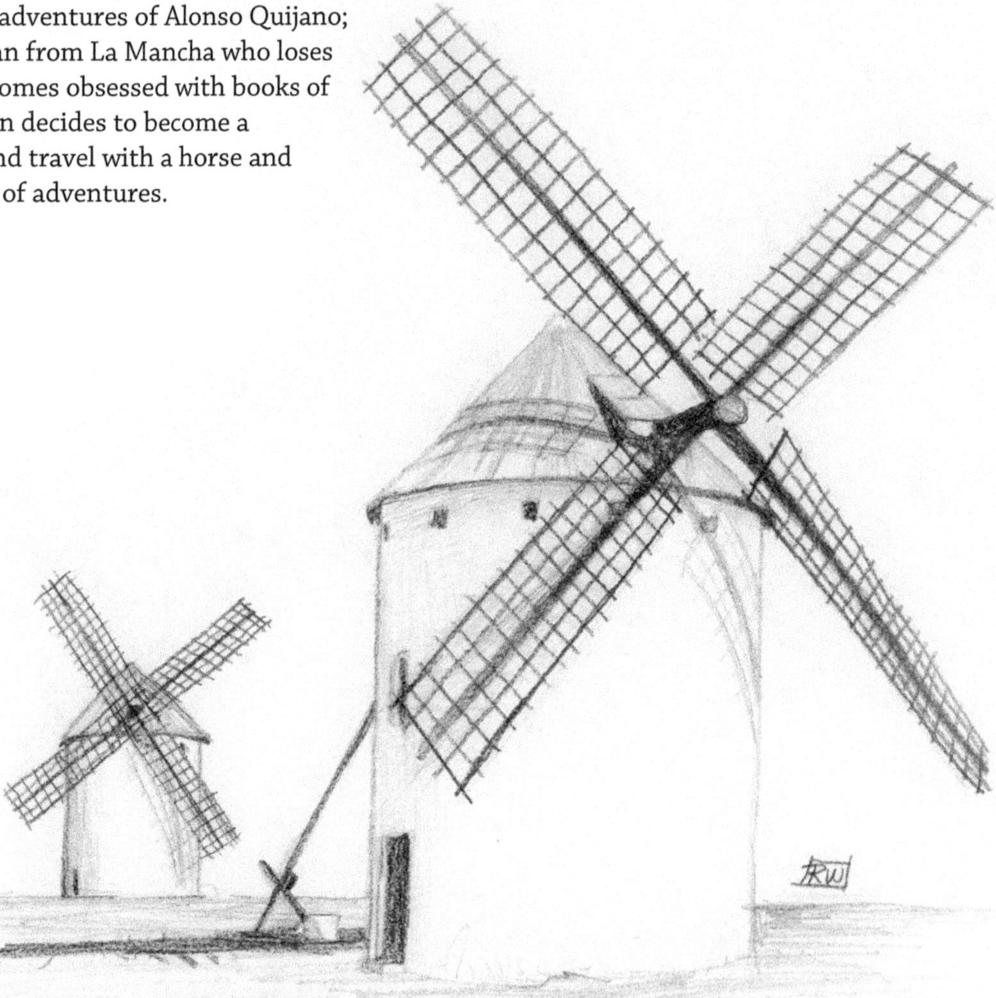

TIP:

Use a variety of weights in your lines by lifting the pencil or pressing harder.

Windmill & Tulips of the Netherlands

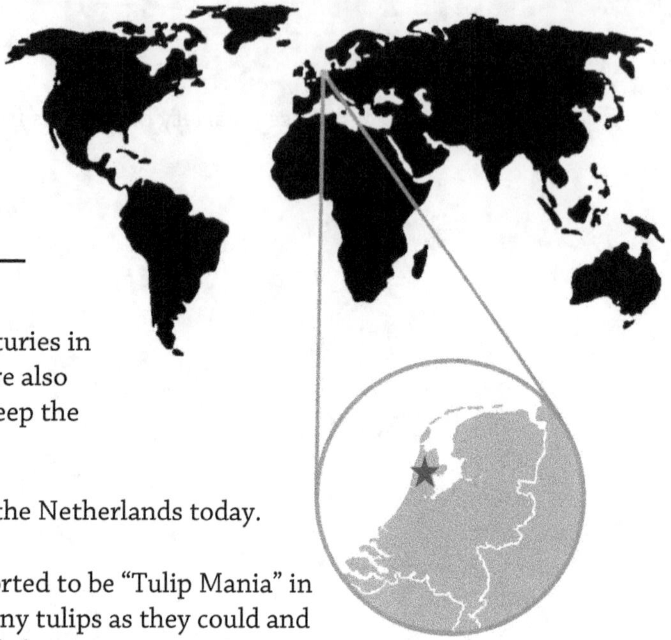

- Windmills and watermills have been used for centuries in the Netherlands to grind grain for flour. They were also used for pumping lakes and swamps in order to keep the land dry from flooding.

- There are still over 1,000 water and windmills in the Netherlands today.

- The first economic bubble in world history is reported to be "Tulip Mania" in Amsterdam in the 1630s. People bought up as many tulips as they could and tulip prices went through the roof, until the bubble burst.

- Today, the Netherlands is still the world's main producer of tulips, exporting as many as three billion bulbs annually.

- Tulips are actually edible, and are a distant cousin to the onion!

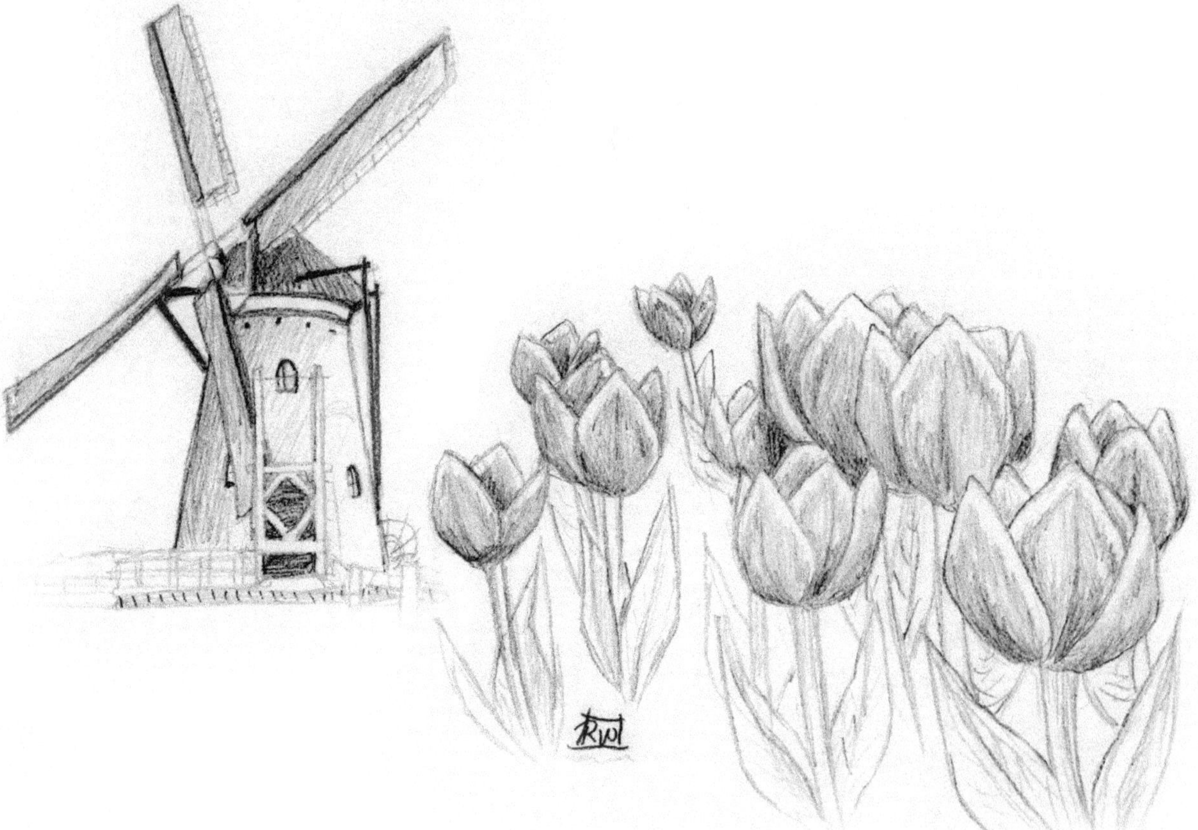

Take your time and use as much detail as you like.
When you have finished, take a step back and appreciate the piece of artwork you have created.

Conclusion

- **Additional Resources:**

Now that you have reached the conclusion of *Around the World in 80 Drawings*, I hope that you enjoyed your time working through the pages, learning exciting facts from locations all around the world, and sketching your own masterpieces using the helpful tips.

If you enjoyed this book, and would like more information on drawing tutorials, resources, and advice for artists of all levels, please check out my website: **http://thingstodraw.org.**

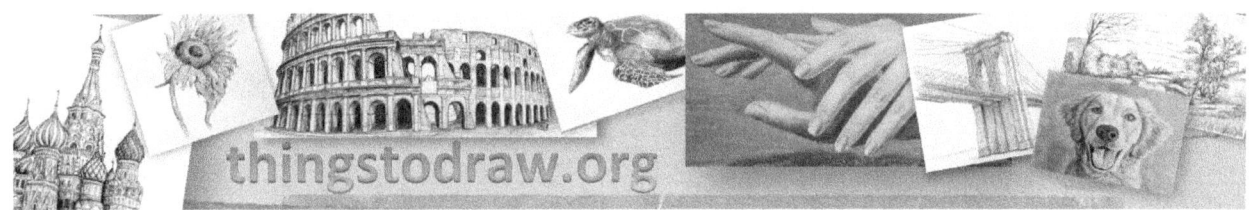